Megan Buskey

Ukraine Is Not Dead Yet

A Family Story of Exile and Return

D1265207

UKRAINIAN VOICES

Collected by Andreas Umland

The book series "Ukrainian Voices" publishes English- and German-language monographs, edited volumes, document collections, and anthologies of articles authored and composed by Ukrainian politicians, intellectuals, activists, officials, researchers, and diplomats. The series' aim is to introduce Western and other audiences to Ukrainian explorations, deliberations and interpretations of historic and current, domestic, and international affairs. The purpose of these books is to make non-Ukrainian readers familiar with how some prominent Ukrainians approach, view and assess their country's development and position in the world. The series was founded, and the volumes are collected by Andreas Umland, Dr. phil. (FU Berlin), Ph. D. (Cambridge), Associate Professor of Politics at the Kyiv-Mohyla Academy and an Analyst in the Stockholm Centre for Eastern European Studies at the Swedish Institute of International Affairs.

Megan Buskey

UKRAINE IS NOT DEAD YET

A Family Story of Exile and Return

Bibliographic information published by the Deutsche Nationalbibliothek

Die Deutsche Nationalbibliothek lists this publication in the Deutsche Nationalbibliografie; detailed bibliographic data are available in the Internet at http://dnb.d-nb.de.

Bibliografische Information der Deutschen Nationalbibliothek

Die Deutsche Nationalbibliothek verzeichnet diese Publikation in der Deutschen Nationalbibliografie; detaillierte bibliografische Daten sind im Internet über http://dnb.d-nb.de abrufbar.

ISBN-13: 978-3-8382-1691-1

© *ibidem*-Verlag, Stuttgart 2023

Printed in the United States of America

For my family –
past, present, and future

Mazur Family Tree

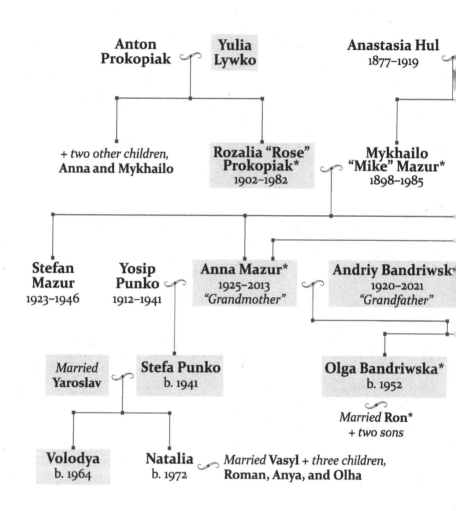

Anton Prokopiak ⌇ **Yulia Lywko**

Anastasia Hul
1877–1919

+ two other children, **Anna and Mykhailo**

Rozalia "Rose" Prokopiak*
1902–1982 ⌇ **Mykhailo "Mike" Mazur***
1898–1985

Stefan Mazur
1923–1946

Yosip Punko ⌇
1912–1941

Anna Mazur*
1925–2013
"Grandmother" ⌇

Andriy Bandriwsk
1920–2021
"Grandfather"

Married **Yaroslav** ⌇ **Stefa Punko**
b. 1941

Olga Bandriwska*
b. 1952

⌇

Married **Ron***
+ two sons

Volodya
b. 1964

Natalia
b. 1972 ⌇ *Married* **Vasyl** *+ three children,*
Roman, Anya, and Olha

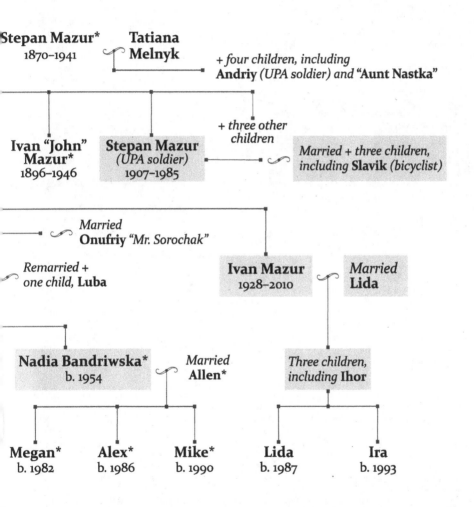

Stepan Mazur* 1870–1941 — Tatiana Melnyk
+ four children, including **Andriy** *(UPA soldier)* and **"Aunt Nastka"**

Ivan "John" Mazur* 1896–1946

Stepan Mazur *(UPA soldier)* 1907–1985

+ three other children

*Married + three children, including **Slavik** (bicyclist)*

Married **Onufriy** *"Mr. Sorochak"*

Remarried + one child, **Luba**

Ivan Mazur 1928–2010 — *Married* **Lida**

Nadia Bandriwska* b. 1954 — *Married* **Allen***

*Three children, including **Ihor***

Megan* b. 1982

Alex* b. 1986

Mike* b. 1990

Lida b. 1987

Ira b. 1993

Gray box denotes residence in Siberia
* *Asterisk denotes residence in the U.S.*

Contents

Prologue

In February 2022, the omicron variant of COVID-19 had swept across the United States, shuttering all the places I frequented as an urban thirtysomething — restaurants, coffee shops, bars, music venues. People rarely ventured from their homes. I made myself walk along the Brooklyn waterfront every day so I could feel the sun on my skin rather than just the glare of the computer screen. The days had the agonizing slowness of previous COVID waves, but February felt particularly ominous. Pulsing beneath the stillness of this second pandemic winter was the drumbeat of possible war.

The news was full of the fact that Russia had amassed more than 100,000 troops along Ukraine's borders. The U.S. government was warning with growing urgency that Russia intended to use this force to launch a full-scale attack on Ukraine. To me, a Ukrainian American with many family members in the country, the news was alarming, to put it mildly. Unthinkable. Bombs falling on the Kyiv neighborhood I had lived in when I was twenty-two? Rockets pounding the steppe that surrounded my grandmother's native village? Russian warships firing at Odesa, where my aunt vacationed each summer with her grandchildren?

I nervously checked in with my family in Ukraine to see what they were thinking. My cousin Lida told me about civil defense groups that had sprung up in Lviv, the city in western Ukraine where she lived and worked as a human resources specialist. Average citizens — teachers, IT programmers, university students — were getting training on how to load guns, apply tourniquets, navigate around mines. "Deep inside, I believe an invasion won't happen," Lida said over Zoom from her apartment, where she was isolating with a suspected case of COVID. Other family members evinced the same belief. Yet each day the news suggested that we were drawing closer to a cataclysm beyond anyone's imagining.

The third Monday of February, I made my morning cup of black tea and milk and checked my Twitter feed, as had become my ritual. The week before, an American magazine had reported that the Russians had drawn up "target and kill lists" of Ukrainians to imprison, torture, deport, and murder as part of their planned occupation. At the time, it had seemed farfetched. Now I read that a senior U.S. government official had described Russia's plans for Ukraine as "extremely violent" and confirmed the accuracy of the magazine's report. "This will not be some conventional war between two armies," the official warned. "It will be waged by Russia on the Ukrainian people—to repress them, crush them, to harm them."

The official's characterization lit a fear in me that none of the previous coverage had. The faces of family members, friends, and former colleagues who might be on the Russians' lists flashed through my mind. They were all people who worked hard, devoted their talents to just causes, had hopes and dreams and flaws and families. The thought that their life's work might be destroyed, that they might be deprived of their freedom, perhaps even their lives, lodged a rock in my stomach.

What made that feeling even more wrenching was that, like many of their countrymen, my own family had been persecuted for being Ukrainian. When I thought of people I knew who could be at risk, their faces merged with the image I had of my grandmother at twenty-five, her face smudged with coal dust from working in the mines after the Soviets exiled her to Siberia for the offense of being related to a Ukrainian nationalist. That such a parallel could occur today shook me far past the point of tears, and I cried hard that morning.

I would cry more in the weeks to come, but that was the moment when I started to grasp the horror of what lay ahead.

By the time Russian president Vladimir Putin gave a lengthy address on the Ukraine "matter" later that day, my tears had dried. Numbness had set in. I scowled at my computer screen as Putin held forth like a drunk, belligerent uncle at Thanksgiving dinner, slouching in his chair, waving his hand imperiously.

Putin's rhetoric was all over the place. He was concerned about the Donbas, a coal-rich region of eastern Ukraine coveted by Moscow. Ukraine was indistinguishable from Russia, its existence

a strategic error committed by Lenin. It was now time to correct
Lenin's mistake, to "decommunize" Ukraine for real. Kyiv had sto-
len gas from Russia. Ukraine was being run as an American puppet
state. Russian-language speakers were being suppressed. Ukraine
was going to develop nuclear weapons. NATO was going to use
Ukraine to attack Russia. Aggressive nationalism and neo-Nazism
had been "elevated in Ukraine to the rank of national policy."

This was not the first time Putin had trotted out this motley
set of arguments. In fact, he had been making these claims for years.
In 2014 he had condemned the pro-European protestors on Kyiv's
central square, Maidan Nezalezhnosti, as "nationalists, neo-Nazis,
Russophobes, and anti-Semites." They had "resorted to terror,
murder, and riots" to seize power, Putin said. "These ideological
heirs of Bandera, Hitler's accomplice during World War II…flaunt
slogans about Ukraine's greatness, but they are the ones who did
everything to divide the nation. Today's civil standoff is entirely on
their conscience."

In the years that followed, he returned to these points again
and again. Putin was clearly preoccupied, if not obsessed, with
Ukraine's existence as an independent state. Twisting the country's
complex history to his own ends, he settled on the message that
Ukraine needed to be "de-Nazified."

The claim was preposterous. For starters, the country was
now led by Volodymyr Zelensky, one of the world's few Jewish
heads of state. Still, I understood, on some level, how that history
could still be felt to be pressing on the present. My family's fraught
history in Ukraine featured many of the same factors — Nazi influence, Ukrainian nationalism, Moscow's imperialism — that Putin
was invoking to justify the invasion. I knew that their interplay was
complicated.

When Russian missiles began to rain down on Ukraine on February 24, that nuance was buried under the rubble and carnage, like
many other aspects of Ukrainian life before the invasion. Russia's
war on Ukraine was the most shocking and devastating geopoliti-
cal act in Europe in more than a generation. And it would bring me
closer to my family story than I ever thought possible.

1
Memory Traces

Throughout my childhood, my brothers and I would periodically gather some of our clothes to put in the packages my grandmother sent to Ukraine. After we completed the first pass, my mother would redo our efforts, getting on her knees so she could get at the overstuffed bottom drawers at the far reaches of our closets. A middle-class family in a Rust Belt suburb, we had no shortage of things. We were especially flush with clothes — they multiplied quickly over the course of a summer, with a new shirt for each sports team and cheap cotton pullovers amassed like puddles in the living room in the aftermath of a birthday party. My mother would take the most undersized and neglected of these garments to my grandmother's house, and my grandmother would add them to the large cardboard box she was preparing to send.

These belongings passed out of my mind quickly. But occasionally they surfaced later, when, out of boredom, I would study photographs of my Ukrainian relatives at my grandmother's house. As I looked at the images of these poker-faced strangers and tried to recall their names and their relation to me, I would feel sparks of recognition: That was my sweater with the rainbow stripes! That was my sweatshirt with the neon-pink bows!

And who would be wearing them but some unsmiling young girl with straight blonde hair and green eyes, like me.

My youthful interest in the photos did not extend beyond these momentary flashes of the uncanny. After all, I was living my childhood at some remove from the culture my mother had come from. I was aware that she was Ukrainian and that she had been born and raised in what we knew as Russia. I knew those places were different, but if anyone had asked me, I would have struggled to explain how. Only well into my adolescence did the matter start to become clear: Siberia was where my mother spent her childhood because my grandmother had been exiled there from her village in Ukraine during the Second World War.

Still, the details were fuzzy. I demurred freshman year when a college classmate asked me whether my grandmother's exile had been under the auspices of the gulag system; the gulag was, like many things at the time, something about which I was not only unschooled but unaware. I did not know that my family was one of the millions in the former Soviet Union who found themselves at the mercy of that system in the twentieth century; I did not know that while conditions in exile had improved over the years, and reached a meager stability by 1954, the year my mother was born, they were as bleak and punishing as the worst of the gulag's labor camps had been when my grandmother arrived there seven years earlier. I had no idea of the complex factors that had led to my family being shunted into that system. And I did not know that the packages that we sent our family in Ukraine were not a thoughtful habit of my grandmother but a long-standing family practice — in place before my grandmother came to the United States, before she was exiled to Siberia, before she was born, in all likelihood.

A constant presence in our lives, our grandmother could have told me all about our family's past, but the differences in our languages and cultural referents made this knowledge almost impossible for her to relay. By the time I was in the thick of grade school, she had retired from her job as a factory worker and was spending two afternoons a week studying the *Cleveland Plain Dealer* at our kitchen table, keeping an eye on us while our mother did her rounds as a physical therapist.

My youngest brother, Mike, was still a toddler then, and my grandmother often spent the early afternoon hours with him at the local park, helping him throw stale bread crusts at the ducks that ambled around its algae-laden pond. For me and my other brother, Alex, four years my junior, my grandmother prepared little crepes ahead of time and brought them over in clear plastic produce bags from the grocery store that bubbled up with steam from the cooked dough. When Alex and I returned from school, we ate the crepes with Aunt Jemima's, then turned our attention to the television. If she hadn't had time to make us a snack beforehand, my grandmother would offer to buckle all of us into her navy Oldsmobile and drive us a mile to the nearest McDonald's. Alex or I ordered because she didn't like to speak English in public.

To do more than that was difficult because she was locked away from us, and us from her, by her limited command of English and the vast distance separating her from the culture that informed our daily lives.

My brothers and I lived in the America my father was born in and my mother had embraced upon arriving from Siberia at the age of twelve—an America that was as sterile as it was in thrall to the popular, and devoid, it seemed, of much history of any kind. Our father, a podiatrist, had been raised by a single mother in a blue-collar neighborhood in the city and, like my mother, wanted a better life for his kids. In our suburb west of Cleveland, the land was cheap, the houses new, the strip malls plentiful, and the culture emphatically incurious. The passage of years could be measured by how much of the area's thick tangle of brown forest had been razed to make way for new roads and subdivisions. The houses in these subdivisions were increasingly large and elaborately windowed, and sat on treeless lots, unshielded from the weak Ohio sun.

Yet there was some gift in the blandness. Sometimes I would walk our dog to the soccer field at the end of our street at night. Even though the field was abutted by roads and whizzing cars on two sides, it was edged on the other sides by a thin stand of trees. The smell of the grass and the melodic hush of the wavering branches had a pleasing, almost magic quality. In other words, there was enough space there—physical and mental—for a kid to dream.

Our mother was foreign, we knew—our grandmother had a normal name, *Anna*, but our mother's name, *Nadia*, had an exotic tinge, and then there was her accent warming and rounding her speech. There were her prominent eyes, heart-shaped face, and full lips, which matched the features of the Russian figure skaters we watched on TV. Even though my mother had spent her formative years outside the United States, she was as much a partisan of American culture as my brothers and I were. Perhaps that's because my mom and Olga, her older sister by two years, had been in the midst of adolescence when they arrived in the United States — old enough to sense the precariousness of their position while young enough to be molded by other people's ideas about how they could assure their security. In the working-class neighborhood in Cleveland where they settled, they were old enough, too, to focus on hard work, saving for when the other shoe dropped. If you did what everyone else was doing, the belief was, you would be okay, and accordingly my mother became a devoted student of American values, culture, and style in their most popular forms.

In all the important ways — language, religion, culture — my grandmother's life didn't depart much from that of the Old Country. Even in appearance, she channeled a different time and land. She carefully draped a sheer babushka over her short, thick white hair and tied it beneath her chin with crooked fingers; wore a thick cross around her neck, its gold tinged with red; attired herself formally in understated dresses and sharply-pressed slacks. Her posture was straight and her shoulders unrounded, as if she were walking on a never-ending tightrope. My mom always referred to her in English as *Mother*, never *Mom*. Later, I would observe that she used the formal form of *you* when addressing her in Ukrainian — *vy*.

It was to please and honor my grandmother that my mother had us participate in an array of Ukrainian customs. My brothers and I resented these efforts for the simple reason that they departed sharply from what we knew and had been conditioned to want. I attended Ukrainian school every Saturday morning for a few years, where I learned to print my name in Cyrillic and listlessly name a few common household objects in Ukrainian, but I disliked the time in the church hall basement, disliked the faint smell of sauerkraut and the accents of some of the other kids, which reminded me of old people. Eventually, my mother gave in and withdrew me. She didn't even try with my brothers.

We sighed heavily when our mother plunked the familiar plate of my grandmother's pierogis and stuffed cabbage on the kitchen table. We gamely kept our Christmas tree up through January 7, the day our Orthodox church celebrated Christmas, though by then it had a bare, even mournful look, because my brothers and I had long ripped open and made off with the colorful presents once arrayed invitingly around it.

What we dreaded the most, though, was church. One Sunday morning a month, my mother would appear at our bedroom doors at an unfriendly hour and unsympathetically tell us to get up. We whined and dawdled. The shower was in the bathroom off my parents' bedroom, and my mom would frogmarch us there herself if she had to, urging us to move more quickly with sharp knocks on the door. Even so, the hot water always ran out before the last of us had finished up. Then I had to struggle into a dress whose sleeves would invariably be too short for my long arms and put on tights that had a scratchy feeling I hated. My friends were all Catholic or mainline Protestant, and they got to wear whatever they wanted to church, even *jeans*.

Our church was in Parma, a city just over Cleveland's western boundary. My grandmother lived there in a modest brick ranch that was about a twenty-minute drive from our house. The city's name suggests that its early residents had Italian heritage, but by my grandmother's time it was a melting pot of white ethnic minorities, and in her enclave Ukrainians and Poles were the most common. Once our mom got us in the van, I would lean my head against the window and look toward the sky as Casey Kasem's Top 40 countdown blared from the radio. The view flickered from the green of tree branches to hazy smokestacks to spindly electrical wires suspended between wooden poles. I'd know my mother had taken the right exit off the freeway as soon as the flags for the used car lot appeared, along with the signs for a nearby cluster of mattress stores, and the hint of onion domes further down State Road that belonged to the area's Serbian, Russian, and Ukrainian churches.

St. Vladimir's held two services on Sundays — the first in English, at 9 a.m., and the second in Ukrainian, at 10:30. As a rule, we attended the Ukrainian service because it was later, even though only my mom could understand what was being said. We often arrived so late that we had to stand at the back wall for a while until we could inconspicuously scoot over to the second to last pew on the left, where my grandmother always stood. The sight of her head turning her head and smiling happily at us as we filed into the pew next to her is one of the most potent memories of my childhood.

The church had an exoticism and beauty that could impress even the grumpiest child. The sandstone building was topped with a copper onion dome that glinted on sunny mornings. The priest paced at the front of the church chanting the ancient liturgy, a smoking thurible of incense swinging from his grip. The voices of the choir thundered from an alcove above the pews. Saints with weirdly long, thin fingers peered down at us from paintings on the domed ceiling. The grand interior culminated in an ornate, mul-tipaneled icon screen that separated the nave from the altar. The elevated, otherworldly feeling of the church was unlike anything else we experienced in our lives. Still, we were children, and the wonder that filled us upon entering the church had the lift of sugar, dissipating quickly, and soon my brothers and I, standing against the back wall or in a pew next to our grandmother, would be shift-ing our weight from one foot to the other, resentful that we were there at all.

After the lengthy service was over, we had to submit to one more protracted ritual: kissing the priest's cross. For this we had to file out of the pews and into a line that moved slowly up the aisle to the front of the church. There, a priest proffered the silver cross that hung around his neck to our waiting lips. "Christ is risen," the priest would say to me in English when I finally arrived at the front of the church. "Indeed, he has risen," I would mumble back before I touched my lips against the cool metal of Christ's body prostrate on the cross.

Three altar boys clad in golden robes waited at the end of the procession. Each held a wooden basket. One of the baskets con-tained small cubes of unleavened bread, and I would dip my fin-gers in and grab a few pieces. In our rush to get out the door in the morning we never had time for breakfast and it was always past noon when the service finally ended.

After the service, my grandmother's small, hobbling friends would flock to her like pigeons spying a bread crust. We would wait for her in the church foyer, bundled up in our coats and staring at the rack of thin candles arrayed before a Mary icon as they burned down to their wicks.

Some of her friends looked at us and beamed, as if the sight of grandchildren unleashed a narcotic. Others regarded us with displeasure and told us to stand up straighter, uncross our arms, and stop leaning against the wall where our heads might unintentionally bump a mounted cross. At church, in sum, we were expected to be obedient, polite, and selfless, in keeping with a place that was supposed to be a temple of the best of human nature. It made sense to me that my grandmother made the church the center of her life and attended services without fail; she had a sense of righteousness. It was another thing about her that I never thought to ask about.

September 1987. I was five years old. It was a glorious fall day, the kind where the sun is shining but distant and you are comfortable outside in jeans and no coat. My mother had spent all morning making food for the guests who had come to celebrate my younger brother Alex's first birthday. They sat on lawn chairs in our backyard holding paper plates in one hand and plastic forks in the other. Alex delighted the adults by taking his first steps at the party, stumbling in red OshKosh B'gosh overalls and a pacifier toward my mother's outstretched arms.

Earlier in the afternoon, I had earned praise for helping my brother open his presents, though I did so in part to eye the choicest of his gifts for myself. A pudgy and jubilant Alex quickly took to one of them: a plastic hammer that he started slamming on a wooden block with the regularity of a heartbeat.

"Who got him that thing?" one of the guests asked, then laughed.

I felt a hotness rise in my chest. My grandmother, the giver of the present, was now fussing in the kitchen, probably trying to get the saltiness of the mashed potatoes right. I imagined her anxiously weighing the worthiness of the gift in the aisle of Toys "R" Us. There was no way I was going to let these people sit in our lawn chairs and laugh at her. My time as helper, it turned out, was not over.

"My grandma did," I announced, and gave the tittering guests the evil eye. "He really likes it."

That reaction occasioned another ripple of laughter. It hung in the air for a moment before fading away.

In fact, my mom had purchased the gift and wrapped it, signing the "from" label with my grandmother's name. She kept this going for years at Christmases and birthdays, as my grandmother had simply no idea what to buy us. And as middle-class American children, it would have been inconceivable to us *not* to receive a gift from her.

A desire to protect is just another way of loving, I think, and my brothers and I loved my grandmother intuitively, almost without knowing. Despite her foreignness, she had a gentle, inoffensive quality about her. Her voice was soft, her breath milky, her frame thin. She was eminently dependable, not just in how she cared for us but in her needs and expectations. That made it easy to take her for granted.

Still, I understood early that she was vulnerable. She had something tragic about her, a quality that puzzled me. She was extremely frugal, for one. She worked zealously. She had no interest in fun as I understood it, like going to a baseball game, watching a movie, or getting a milkshake and walking around the mall.

She was also the only person in my family I ever saw cry. Cry about something much sadder than anything I had known—losing her brother, who had died as a young man. Something about this loss pulled at me—I recognized the power of having a brother. A brother was someone whose teeth you watched inch from his gums, whose ear canal you knew the feel of from when you gave him a wet willy. How strange and gutting it would be for this imperative creature to suddenly be gone.

My grandmother had a framed photo of this brother that she displayed in her house. It drew me like a magnet. The black-and-white photo had been taken in a studio. Her brother, Stefan, was wearing a suit, and his hair was combed back. His handsome face was fixed in a solemn expression, one that conveyed a sense of duty and order. He didn't look like the kind of person who would die tragically. How could this have happened?

When we visited my grandmother, I often looked for the photo — she rearranged her mementos periodically, and sometimes she put the photo in a different room. When I found it, I would outline with my finger the sharp corners of her brother's pressed suit and shirt collars, trace the crimp in his hair, and study his deep-set blue eyes, which I knew well from my grandmother's face. He seemed to possess answers to questions that I was just beginning to put into words, like how my grandmother had ever been young enough to have an older brother of his age, what it felt like to die. For a moment, I would feel the power of these questions in the company of his image, and then I would move on. The lure of the photo was strong but indecipherable. I tiptoed into my grandmother's world, only to draw back into my own.

When my grandmother was in her mid-sixties, she married a widower fourteen years her senior who sang baritone in the church choir. He spoke English as haltingly as she did, and at meals, after a few highballs, he would look off into the distance and break out into Ukrainian songs.

Having him in our family was an adjustment. Our grandmother had been single our whole lives. No explanation was given for the absence of her previous husband, my grandfather. My aunt, Olga, urged us to call this short, sharp-kneed replacement *Grandpa*. We refused. Even now, years since he passed, we refer to him as Mr. Sorochak. There was precedence for this resistance, as my grandmother had pleaded with us to refer to her as *Baba*, though the Ukrainian word felt wrong in our mouths and we continued to call her *Grandma*.

Together they took church-sponsored bus trips to Niagara Falls, went to retirement barbecues, funeral receptions, and bingo, and rose before dawn to help make pierogis the church sold as a fundraiser. Like my grandmother, Mr. Sorochak had been an industrious factory worker with modest tastes, at a time when strong unions promised an old age with few worries apart from deciphering Medicare statements. He and my grandmother generously spent their savings on her progeny, particularly us grandchildren and our exorbitant college educations—educations, of course, that they never dreamt of for themselves.

Together they lived in my grandmother's one-story, solid brick house a few blocks from St. Vlad's. The garage was unattached. The grout between the bathroom tiles had become, over time, dark lines of black. There was no automatic disposal or dishwasher, and in good weather my grandmother dried her linens on a thin rope she hung between the back wall of the house and a tree in the middle of the small backyard. Mr. Sorochak carefully maintained the lawn, and cultivated a suite of roses under the bedroom window.

In the summer, my grandmother grew tomatoes, cucumbers, peas, and zucchini in the rows of dirt along the perimeter of the backyard, and when she visited us, she brought us sacks of them along with whatever she had baked recently—cookies with the density of rocks, challah bread, lemon cake. We received these items so frequently that we lost any taste for them, yet she continued to bring them, stacking our refrigerator with foil-topped cake sheets that several days later my mother would reluctantly put in the trash.

"She wants to be sure that we have enough to eat," my mother said to account for my grandmother's prodigious cooking. As an explanation, that rang hollow. Hunger didn't exist in our world. If anything, we had more food than we knew what to do with. Our pantry overflowed with boxes of cereal, jars of spices, unopened bottles of different kinds of oils and vinegars, and bags of so many types of flour that my mother had to line them up on the pantry floor. Our freezer was stacked with frozen Stouffer's lasagna and macaroni and cheese. Our refrigerator was a maze of milk cartons, cups of yogurt and sour cream, and heads of lettuce, cabbage, and cauliflower. In spite of this overwhelming evidence, my grandmother still seemed to worry that we might starve. The concern was yet another reminder of her strangeness and singularity, that she had come from a different place altogether, one governed by different rules.

November 1989. I am seven years old and watching television with my father. On the screen is a broadcast from Berlin. It is nighttime there, and masses of people in winter coats are pushing against a tall metal gate. The gate breaks open and the people stream through the gap, their faces ecstatic.

The broadcast cuts to a scene in a different part of town. There, people are standing on a thick, tall concrete wall. Some are holding sparklers; the neon-hued graffiti scrawled on the wall matches the color of some of the onlookers' pants. A few men are striking at the wall with hammers and mallets, trying to chisel off a piece of the cement.

"I never thought I would see this in my lifetime," my father marvels.

After the fall of the Berlin Wall, I was shown the family photos at my grandmother's house more purposefully. The hope was that now some of the people in these photographs would be able to come to the United States to visit.

When the Soviet Union dissolved in 1991, that hope became a reality. In the summer of 1993, my mother's sister Stefa came, bringing along her daughter Natalia, who at twenty-one was ten years my senior, and her uncle Ivan, my grandmother's only surviving sibling. They had all stayed behind in the Soviet Union for reasons that were then obscure to me, and my grandmother hadn't seen them for more than twenty-five years. She had never met Natalia, her granddaughter.

They knew no English and my brothers and I no Ukrainian, so we were divided from them as if by a thick glass. What I remember from the time is mainly sensory: how dark Stefa's hair seemed against her pale face; how gently Natalia's hands rested on my shoulders; how many fleshy moles bubbled up from Ivan's skin; how a thick, musty smell emanated from the carved wooden boxes they gave to us as presents. I remember that my parents marveled that the three were dumbstruck when they visited our local grocery store, and that they spent hours examining the different items in the aisles. The joke was that Ivan had overestimated our access to the comforts of capitalism and asked my grandmother to buy him a car.

But we could sense the significance of their presence to our grandmother—how animated she became, how much more she laughed and joked. Then, too, there was the resemblance. We dimly understood that Stefa was my grandmother's daughter by her first marriage (my mom and Olga the products of her second), and she bore little similarity to either of her half-sisters. Unlike my mom and Olga, Stefa had small eyes, thin lips, and dark brown hair, which she wore in page-boy style. Natalia had Stefa's dark hair and eyes but she flushed more easily and her nose was rounder.

Ivan, however, was fairer and had the same striking blue eyes as my grandmother and Stefan, their brother in the photograph at my grandmother's house. In fact, to look Ivan in the eyes was to feel a moment of confusion about who you were actually looking at, him or my grandmother, and their resemblance drove home for me as nothing else had that my grandmother had endured something terrible to have lived apart from her closest family for so long.

While they were visiting, we went out to dinner at Red Lobster. It was a step up from our usual fare, and so we donned our stiff church attire. The service at the restaurant was slow, and we spent a long time waiting in the lobby where a couple of lobsters loitered at the bottom of a murky tank, their pinchers bound. For once, our family was large enough to call for a long rectangular table, the head of which my grandmother refused to occupy. Instead, she took a seat in the middle, where she dominated the conversation all the same. I sat at one of the ends with my brothers and cousins, where bin after bin of salty cheddar biscuits was placed before us and summarily consumed.

The next day, our Ukrainian relatives were gone. In my room I found a delicate rose-colored heart ornament, plastic but cut to look like glass, hanging from a tack on my bulletin board—a gesture of warmth, a token of beauty, and a reminder not to forget.

2
Borderland

"*Nu*, Megan, are you going to have another cup of tea?"

My grandmother's large blue eyes peered at me expectantly through her thick-lensed glasses. We were sitting in her kitchen at a small table cluttered with opened envelopes, her address book, a bulky landline phone, and a plate of homemade *kolacky* laden with confectioners' sugar, some of which had wafted onto the table itself. I nodded, and she handed me a packet of Lipton from the box sitting next to the cookies, its paper wrapper so old that it was foxed at the edges.

Afternoons like this were a normal occurrence in the late aughts and early 2010s whenever I visited Cleveland from the East Coast, where I had ended up in my mid-twenties. My relationship with my grandmother had changed a lot since I was a kid. I had left Cleveland at 18 to attend the University of Chicago, whose famed liberal arts curriculum had substantially expanded my horizons and, just as crucially, given me the audacity to believe that I could even go beyond them. No longer did my grandmother's foreignness, her different values, her age, make her seem remote to me. Now those things made her fascinating, unique, and special.

Once I started to take notice, I discovered that it was a delight to spend time with her. While she didn't seek to be the center of attention, she told stories well, with confidence and dramatic poise. She had a good sense of humor. She could be teased and laugh about it. She was extremely frugal, yes, but also admirably skeptical of the enduring value of material things.

It helped, of course, that I now had a working knowledge of Ukrainian. In college, I had thrown myself into learning the language, inspired as much by my university's brazen intellectual spirit, where no learning endeavor was too obscure, as by the possibility of connecting more meaningfully to my heritage.

That meant that these afternoons of togetherness in my grandmother's kitchen, or on the margins of family dinners, now took place in her native language. How she loved to talk: about carrying sacks of potatoes on her back to her family's cellar to store them for the winter; learning Russian in Siberia by studying the newsprint wrapped around the piece of bread she was given each day at the mine; going to the *banya* each night after a shift to scrub off the dark paste of soot and sweat; caroling with other Ukrainians in the exile settlement around the winter holidays, just as they would have if they had still been in their native villages.

"How we caroled," I remember her saying. "Every carol that we knew."

My understanding of my grandmother grew by leaps and bounds during these talks. But my view of her character was not entirely rosy. I saw, for instance, how her temper could fracture under stress. Her main forms of communication with Mr. Sorochak were instructive mumbling and yelling, and she usually instigated the volley of shouts they could rack up over something as innocuous as what to have for lunch. As she got older, she took her weakening grasp of her affairs out on my mom and aunt Olga, who learned to gird themselves for invective when they suggested that she organize her medical bills in a binder rather than a pile of used envelopes or that, given that she had reached her mid-eighties, she allow a hired hand to shovel her driveway when it snowed.

I also was aware that she harbored some retrograde beliefs. Every so often she would make a comment that betrayed ugly attitudes about ethnic groups and minorities. The Russians were, in her estimation, the worst, followed closely by the Poles. A friend's husband was nice — "for a Jew." On a trip home after I had moved to the East Coast for my first job, I left her alone with a few distant relatives at a lunch. When I returned, they looked at me wide-eyed. "Your grandmother was telling us about the concerns she has about you living in New York," one of them said.

"She sure is afraid of black people," another added.

I shrugged these comments off. They caused no real harm, I told myself. They appeared only occasionally, and any old white lady with a limited education might say similar things from time to time.

The truth was that I wanted to be close to her, but on terms that were comfortable for me—which meant avoiding confrontation. This also extended to how I captured her memories. Cleveland was home to a Ukrainian museum, and it launched an oral history project to capture the life stories of Ukrainian Americans in the area. I signed my grandmother up to be interviewed and sat next to her in one of the homey rooms on the museum's first floor as the project director interviewed her about her impoverished childhood, the misery of the war, and her responsibilities in the coal mines of Siberia.

As I drove her home that afternoon, I mentioned that we could go back and talk more if she wanted. She demurred—talking about the past made it difficult to sleep, she said. I didn't push the matter. I respected her feelings and didn't want to cause her pain by forcing her to revisit difficult memories. That conflict created a spell that kept me close to her life story but always at its edges.

By that point, I wasn't just a Ukrainian speaker; I had lived in Ukraine and traveled extensively there. My first experience had come in 2003, when I received a grant from my university to spend a summer learning Ukrainian in situ. I picked a program in picturesque Lviv, a city of soaring steeples and spires in western Ukraine, close to the village my grandmother was from, and eagerly packed my bags. I would be the first member of my American family to visit Ukraine since the early 1990s, when my grandmother and Mr. Sorochak had made a trip with a group from church.

My parents were bemused yet generally supportive of my interest. My mother asked me quizzically why I didn't just study Russian, a "more useful" language. My grandmother seemed to be thrilled, however, and I felt that part of my purpose had been accomplished by that alone.

On my way to the airport for my first flight to Ukraine, I saw my grandmother's number light up on my cell phone. I was surprised to see she was calling—she had never dialed my cell phone before, believing it not possible from a landline. As I held the phone to my ear, I could tell right away that she was crying.

"It's not like here. There are bad people there," she said, speaking in labored English through her tears. I tried to assure her that I would be careful, that I was part of a university program that would monitor my every move. Yet she repeated: *There are bad people there.* Okay, okay. I hung up, mildly annoyed in the way that twenty-year-olds can be when told they are unprepared for the world. It didn't occur to me for a long time that her anxiety might be stemming from something beyond caution, that it was coming from experience that, at the time, I couldn't fathom.

I forgot her words in the bustle of arriving in Ukraine. In my most colorful imaginings, I could not have conjured up a place that could be so vibrant and so broken. Lviv's center seemed drawn from a storybook about genteel Hapsburg Europe, with its wrought-iron railings and cobblestone streets, but its outskirts were dominated by rundown, prefabricated apartment buildings, their cracked and disintegrating facades a powerful symbol of the harshness and neglect suffusing every corner of post-Soviet life. The cars that rumbled through the streets coughed out narrow streams of black smoke. The trunks of trees were inexplicably covered in a chalky white paint, giving them a sickly look. After sunset, the roads were dark because the city lacked the means to light the streetlamps at night.

A river, the Poltva, had once flowed through Lviv, but it had been diverted and buried during the nineteenth century because of the threat of malaria. More than 150 years later, this meant that tap water was only available six hours a day, from six to nine in the morning and six to nine in the evening. Everyone kept gigantic tubs in reserve in their apartments in the likely event that the utilities failed to keep even that schedule. Arranged around them were large jugs of drinking water purchased at the market or filled at a public well, because the water that did flow from the tap was not potable.

The roads were riddled with potholes, the drivers reckless and fond of speed. Over the course of the summer, I passed by the

aftermath of three car crashes where motionless bodies lay unat-
tended. When I went for a run in a park by the university, a young
girl playing with her barking dog stared at me and then called out.
"You can't run around like that," her eyes hard. "You're bothering
the dog."

My Ukrainian language teacher was a woman in her thirties
with porcelain skin and pretty hazel eyes. Bright and hard-work-
ing, she had completed her *kandydat nauk*, a qualification roughly
equivalent to a doctorate in the American academic system. Even
so, she felt deeply dissatisfied with her life. For years she had been
frustrated by her low salary, her cramped apartment, the water ra-
tioning, the labyrinthine bureaucracy. "I am nothing but a slave of
this country," she soberly told our class one afternoon, and I felt the
weight of Ukraine's poverty in a new way.

Yet, for all of its hardships, there was still something intoxi-
catingly real about the place. People strolled along cobblestone
streets to the ornate opera house, drank coffees served on doilies,
attended churches whose liturgies hadn't changed in hundreds of
years. There were no sprinkler systems, no overhead fluorescent
lighting, no things that beeped or buzzed at you, no runners jog-
ging by in neon-colored clothing. Smells came at you unfiltered,
unprocessed, bracing, and earthy. Most people still shopped for
their daily needs at markets, where they haggled with farmers who
came in from the surrounding villages with their harvest, or in the
small but strangely roomy groceries where products were kept behind walls of glass, as in Soviet times.

Lviv was dense with meaning, and even then I understood
that that was partly because of its complicated history. I had a
grade-schooler's fascination with sites associated with the Second
World War—not surprisingly, as the war had been a staple of my
education since childhood. My Cleveland suburb regularly hosted
a visiting theater troupe whose seeming purpose was to impart lessons to us schoolchildren about every human act of mass barbarity.
The Holocaust was always foremost among them. Serious and sensitive, I was the perfect audience for these earnest productions and
easily absorbed their black-and-white portrayal of history.

I was surprised to find that in a city where the Holocaust had actually taken place, elaborate hallowedness was in short supply. After class one afternoon, I spent more than an hour walking to the site of the Janowska concentration camp, the region's largest, on the outskirts of Lviv. Once I got there, I found only a locked fence and a commemorative rock the size of the ancient Soviet Ladas that still motored noisily through the city's streets. Another site, the entrance to the former Jewish ghetto, had something more along the lines of what I was expecting: a massive black statue of a flailing man raising his arms to the sky, the body abstracted but his anguish clear. Yet there were no educational placards in the humble plaza that surrounded the statue, nothing showing the geographical bounds of the ghetto, no specifics about the people who had been incarcerated there or what they had endured.

Ukraine's poverty was rapidly teaching me to adjust my expectations for what a society could furnish. I understood that historical commemoration and education were luxuries compared with things like staffed hospitals, a reliable electrical grid, and public busses that didn't break down. But I couldn't shake the feeling that the neglect had other causes besides a lack of funds. In the heart of the city languished the ruins of a synagogue targeted for destruction by the Nazis during the war. There was a small plaque mounted on one of the synagogue's few surviving walls, but it commanded little respect. I learned from locals, and verified myself, that the ruins functioned mainly as a place for dog owners to take their pets to relieve themselves.

I wasn't yet curious about where my family fit into this story of the past. I was still trying to wrap my head around all that Ukraine was in the present. On the streets of Lviv, I saw women who reminded me of my grandmother all the time. Most of them sat on stools near the curb, where they watched over a tarp arrayed with root vegetables or a bucket filled with sunflower seeds. Often they pleaded aggressively with passersby, hurling the name and price of an item of produce at you. Some of them were quieter, and if I stopped to buy something, they smiled at me and clasped my hand for a moment after they gave me my change.

It struck me over and over again that it was only due to a twist of fate that my grandmother was not seated with them.

After the language program in Lviv ended, I spent a few weeks with my aunt Stefa, my mother's eldest sister. My relatives in Ukraine had been overjoyed at my arrival. By then, I had come to understand that my family had been separated by the Soviet Union's draconian exit visa policy: In the 1960s, my grandmother had received an exit visa to immigrate to the United States, which her minor daughters, my mom and Olga, could travel on. (All three of them are literally squeezed into the photo in my grandmother's Soviet passport.) By that point, Stefa was in her twenties and married, and was not granted an exit visa herself. After returning from Siberia in the 1960s, she had settled with her husband, Yaroslav, and their young son, Volodya, in Truskavets, a sleepy town in the foothills of the Carpathian Mountains known for its curative mineral waters. My cousin Natalia was born there in the early 1970s.

Stefa's father had died when she was a baby, so technically she was my mother's half-sister. That connection was moot, though, as no relationship had been maintained with Stefa's father's family. If anything, Stefa had been more like a parent than sister to my mom and Olga, given that she was more than ten years older than them and my grandmother had to work in the mines six days a week. During their shared childhood in Siberia, Stefa had been the one who braided her sisters' long hair, walked them to school, pulled their legs up when the mud on the unpaved streets sucked at their booted feet.

My mom had not wanted to leave Siberia, Stefa liked to remind me. When it came time to say goodbye, my mother, then twelve years old, had cried and clung to Stefa.

I quickly understood what it would have been like to have been one of Stefa's charges. I had only met my aunt once before, when she had visited the United States more than a decade earlier. Now, in Ukraine, Stefa looked after me as if I were the same small girl she had first met in Cleveland. She nervously watched me during meals, urged me to help myself to plates of food that she somehow seemed to think I had not seen with my own eyes. "Megan, have a potato," she would say. "Eat a cutlet," she would order, pointing her fork at a pile of fried, egg-battered chicken slices. A few minutes later: "Take a tomato." More often she would simply say, "Megan, eat." Polite initially, I eventually started to answer her commands with stony silence. "The child does not want to eat," Stefa would moan to herself while I avoided her eyes.

Every time I mentioned "Americans," Stefa made a half-moon around her waist with her arms. "Fat," she would then say seriously, as if she were disclosing a secret I was ignorant of. "We have natural food here," Stefa said once when I rolled my eyes at this, drawing out the word *natural* and looking pointedly at me.

I got along well with her daughter, my cousin Natalia, who lived close to Stefa in a one-bedroom apartment with her husband, Vasyl, and their school-aged son, Roman, whom they affectionately called Romchik. Barely thirty, Natalia had an easy way about her that I remembered from her visit to the United States, even though a moat of language difference had separated us. One Saturday morning, Vasyl took Roman along with him while he ran errands, and Natalia and I spent two hours draped in heavy fleece blankets aimlessly watching home movies of her honeymoon in Egypt. The connection between us was warm and effortless, and it made me wonder how my life would have been different if Natalia and I had grown up in the same country.

Stefa was constantly thinking of ways to entertain me, sending me on a guided tour of the city; taking me to a concert by one of her favorite singers, a plump middle-aged crooner who accepted carnations from male audience members as she sang; cajoling Natalia and Vasyl into taking me on a hike in the Carpathian Mountains.

One weekend Stefa brought me to the wedding reception for a family friend. The celebration took place on an outdoor terrace, where tables draped in white cloth were topped with elaborate spreads of meats, cheeses, fish, vegetables, and salads thick with mayonnaise. We took a seat at a table where Stefa knew a few people. Amid their intimate back-and-forth, I quickly grew bored. I concentrated on a plate of raw vegetables and salmon, and made a game of twisting just one or two drops of juice from a lemon slice onto the pale orange fish before I ate it. I consumed a truckload of raw vegetables and salmon in this manner. To this day, I can't look at raw salmon without thinking about this wedding.

Eventually I grew restless and got to my feet and walked around the terrace. The bride and groom, just a year or two older than my twenty-one, sat side by side at a long table in the front of the space, barely looking at each other. I noticed a thoroughfare beyond the terrace, and ventured down it, enjoying the momentary quiet and the green of the trees.

I was a good three hundred feet from the building when I heard Stefa calling from behind me. I turned and saw her hurrying down the gravel path, her hand beckoning to me.

An exchange about my freedom of movement ensued. I didn't follow the meaning of Stefa's words exactly, but surmised that I stood the risk of being raped on this pleasant path and I needed to come back to the table. Tears sprang to my eyes as I struggled to explain that back home I lived on my own and was able to come and go as I pleased. Stefa looked nervous about crossing me, but her anxiety won out. "It's different here," she said solemnly. I needed to come back to the group. Reluctantly, I did.

I sat sullenly at the table as the night stretched on. Eventually, some of my table mates coaxed me onto the dance floor, and in spite of myself, I enjoyed it. But as the clock ticked closer to 2 a.m., I pulled on Stefa's elbow; I was tired and wanted to leave. I thought we had stayed more than long enough, but disappointment was evident on Stefa's face. She nodded but checked with me a few minutes later: I still wanted to go? I assented and she stood up from the table. "The child wants to leave," she told her friends, who looked up from their absorbed conversations with surprise.

By the end of that summer, I had a working knowledge of the language that had floated around me all of my childhood. More importantly, I had met many of the people whose presences had flickered in my life from photos and conversation for just as long. There was Stefa's son, my cousin Volodya, a handsome masseur who applied his fingers of steel to the backs of vacationers who came to Truskavets to avail themselves of the mineral waters; my grandmother's brother Ivan, who materialized as a grayer, feebler version of the man I remembered from a decade earlier, but who still had the same striking eyes as my grandmother; my second cousins Lida and Ira, who were a few years younger than me and with whom I shared the same shade of sandy-blonde hair; my mom's cousin Ihor, a kindly engineer who lived in a Kyiv high-rise with his spirited wife, Tanya, and a demonic cat named Raspberry; Olha (there were many Olhas), the wife of my mother's cousin, who called and wrote my grandmother with such frequency that she spoke of Olha as if she were living down the street, not halfway around the world. And on and on—so many friendly faces, eager to greet me and feed me; delighted that I had become interested in Ukraine and could hazard some conversation in the language; curious about my life and my family in the United States and especially how my grandmother, Mom, and Olga were faring. The experience was overwhelming but warm—warm in a way that had the close, firm hold of family.

Yet I had been shaken by all I had seen—the dilapidated apartment buildings; the purple-faced men reeking of booze as they walked unsteadily down the street; the dead bodies left lying in wrecked cars, no ambulance personnel in sight. Back in the United States that fall, I found myself saddled with ambient anxiety I had never experienced before. My boyfriend was in India at the time, and as I slept alone in my apartment at night I dreamt that his car had tumbled off the sharp switchbacks he described negotiating in the Himalayas. During the day, the wind was so strong it seemed to be smothering me. I worried that I was again suffering from asthma, which I had been tentatively diagnosed with as a teenager. Once, riding the subway, I became convinced that my windpipe was on the verge of closing completely. I got off the train halfway to my destination, hurried to the nearest pharmacy, and bought an inhaler. I rested on the dirty gray carpet in a quiet corner until I felt jittery enough to believe that the medicine was working.

Eventually it dawned on me that my experiences might have psychological, not medical, causes. I made an appointment at the student health center with a therapist who confirmed my suspicions. As soon as I realized that I was causing the panic myself, the feeling stopped.

Ukraine, it is commonly observed, means "borderland" in the Ukrainian and Russian languages. This meaning is often invoked to explain that Ukrainian territory has long served as a buffer between cultures, whether between Christendom and the Islamic world in the Middle Ages, or Europe and Russia more recently.

I came to think of Ukraine as representing a borderland of my own, a psychic one. Before I had gone to Ukraine, my view of the world was fixed. I had assumed that certain things were immutable: People greeted each other with care. Certain boundaries — time, space, independence — were respected. If you were sick, you could get help. Your apartment building was whole; your lights burned at your command; water flowed freely from faucets.

Now I possessed personal experience that had proved that assumption false. I had crossed into a new understanding of how the world worked; Ukraine had revealed to me a glimmer of the unjust suffering it could hold. With this new awareness, I tightened inside. Mild acts of subversion — partying, culling a hip wardrobe from thrift store bins, sarcasm — lost their allure. I became kinder as I understood in a new way that people could not help the circumstances they were born into. I now understood that circumstances alone could be crushing. Perhaps one way of accounting for this change was simply to say that I was becoming an adult. But I also felt that visiting Ukraine had been crucial to this understanding, and that there was still more for me to learn.

After I graduated from college in 2004, I returned to Ukraine and stayed for a year on a Fulbright fellowship. My time there coincided with the Orange Revolution, a heady moment in Ukrainian history when massive public protests helped overturn a rigged presidential election. Witnessing the event was my first real political education. It opened my mind to fresh ways of thinking about all kinds of social problems: the woes of post-Soviet economies, the selective application of the rule of law, the unequal access to quality health care. Armed with these new perspectives, I started to think about how these wrongs could be righted, and how I could take part.

When I came back to the United States, I took a series of jobs that eventually led me to a policy position at a development-focused foundation in the nation's capital, where, using the imperfect tools of briefing books and strategic plans, I sought to leverage my passion into something useful.

Sometimes, though, when I looked at my Outlook inbox for long stretches, an inner voice whispered to me that I wasn't doing much of anything at all.

My grandmother died in the first weeks of the spring of 2013. She was eighty-eight, so it feels strange to call her death unexpected, but its cause—a heart attack or stroke that struck in the middle of the night, causing her to collapse in the bathroom—came on without warning. Mr. Sorochak, whom she had outlived by eight years, had died at ninety-seven, and we had all expected her to follow the model of his long decline, growing slower and feebler by the year, collapsing into herself so much that she finally became still, like a stone. She did not. To the end of her days, my grandmother was vibrant; she kept her agency and her spirit until, all at once, they left her.

Her death struck me like a thunderbolt. How could this beloved person, this seemingly permanent feature of life, suddenly be gone? How could her vitality be extinguished? How could her story be over? How?

My grandmother had arranged and paid for her own funeral many years earlier, so my mom, Olga, and I didn't have those logistics to distract us in the days after her death. To keep busy, we threw ourselves into going through her belongings; the modest brick ranch house in Parma she had so carefully tended would have to be sold eventually. While my grandmother was tidy, she had lived in the house for decades and inherited the belongings of her parents, so we had quite a task before us.

My grandmother had a habit of storing papers in used mailing envelopes, on which she would scrawl descriptions of their contents in Ukrainian. The envelopes suggested she was interested in maintaining some kind of order, but in truth they were just vessels for her clutter — receipts for packages she sent to Ukraine, a bewildering number of icon cards from funerals (what was it like to lose so many friends?), bills from Medicare, a Ukrainian newspaper from the nineties. Once my mother opened a used envelope to find a thousand dollars still wrapped in a tie from the bank.

The envelopes that thrilled me the most contained old photographs. We marveled that there were so many of them that we hadn't seen, the oldest ones crimped along their white borders, as photos once commonly were. When I found a photo of her, I felt a tingle of pleasure and studied it closely. My opportunities to have new experiences with her were dwindling. This was a way to stay close.

When I had exhausted the photos, I found myself pursuing that closeness in other ways. I finagled reading privileges at a nearby university library so I could read specialized books about my grandmother's time and region that were too costly to buy. I wrote archives in Poland and Ukraine to request documents pertaining to my family. During meetings at work, I positioned my laptop so I could scroll unnoticed through passenger lists from Ellis Island. I dusted off recordings of the interviews I had done with my grandmother over the years, and had them transcribed and translated into English so I could understand all of their nuances.

A few months after I started down this path, I visited the ivy-clad Freud Museum in London. I stopped short at a quote on one of the walls from Virginia Woolf in which she explained that her novel *To the Lighthouse* had been fueled by her fixation with her mother, who died when the author was thirteen:

> When it was written, I ceased to be obsessed by my mother. I no longer hear her voice; I do not see her.... I suppose that I did for myself what psychoanalysts do for their patients. I expressed some very long and deeply felt emotion. And in expressing it I explained it and then laid it to rest.

I didn't recognize the feeling of resolution, but the compulsive need to describe I knew. In my previous forays into my grandmother's life, I had not gone far enough. I needed to know more. And if her story was going to be truly preserved and remembered, I had a lot of work to do.

3

Frail Like Straw

One morning some time after my trip to London, I watched as the faded green brush of rural Ukraine streamed by my car window. I was about seventy miles southwest of Lviv. The blue peaks of the Carpathian Mountains beckoned in the distance. It was spring, and the clouds were temperamental, tumbling across the sky and gauzing up the sun. Daylight lasted almost two hours longer in Ukraine this time of year than on the East Coast, where I was visiting from, and I felt the mental lift of impending summer.

The telltale markers of post-Soviet urban life — hulking, prefab apartment buildings; elegant porticos dating back to the Austro-Hungarian Empire, mired in grime; neon advertisements touting cafés, beer, and groceries — had vanished miles earlier. The scene before me would have been familiar to centuries of visitors to the region. Fields in various stages of bloom extended from both sides of a road pocked with potholes. Farmers with long-handled hoes hunched over the land, their arms, legs, and necks already browned by the spring sun. The men wore hats to shield their faces; the women, bandanas to keep their hair back. The farmers pulled at the earth with vigor, churning soil known for being the blackest and most fertile in Europe. One of the women in the fields was heavily pregnant, but she stooped at her work like the others, her swollen belly disappearing in the fold at her waist.

Since the beginning of the drive, the land had been flat; fields of corn, wheat, and barley quilted the horizon. Now, in the distance, the foothills of the mountains slowly began to take shape. When I caught sight of the coruscating crosses topping the three-domed church perched at the summit of the one of the highest hills, I knew we were nearing our destination. The village church as sentinel.

We had arrived: Staryava, the village where my grandmother grew up.

I had come to the village that day thanks, as always, to Stefa, who had conscripted my cousin Natalia's patient husband, Vasyl, into driving us from Truskavets. Staryava was only about thirty miles as the crow flew from Stefa's apartment, but it still took us about an hour and a half to get there on account of the crummy rural roads.

Vasyl was reputed to be the best driver in the family. He demonstrated his bona fides that morning by ably weaving the car around not just potholes but other common features of the Ukrainian countryside: a horse-drawn wagon carrying towers of hay bales; an elderly man peddling doggedly atop a wobbly bike, a cigarette hanging from his mouth; chickens running loose on the shoulder of the road, pecking at the loose gravel for food.

Like my grandmother and innumerable generations of the family before her, Stefa had been born in Staryava. She hadn't lived there since the age of six, though, when she was exiled to Siberia along with my grandparents. As our family's de facto matriarch in Ukraine, Stefa kept tabs on the extended family who remained in the village, along with others who lived throughout the country. Each time I visited, I came in Stefa's company because she knew everyone and everyone knew her.

I had visited Staryava for the first time as a college student and returned when I could, drawn both by the vexed connection born of my grandparents' exile from the place and its beautiful, eerie magic. Natalia joked that I had been there more times than she had, though she lived thirty miles away and I more than five thousand.

There were obvious reasons I found Staryava alluring. Nestled in the foothills of the Eastern Beskids, a range of the Carpathian Mountains, the village looked as if it had been conceived by a painter. The foothills were composed of layers of exquisite color. Dark knobs of spruce crowned their summits, while the hillsides themselves had been cleared for fields that ran the gamut of natural hues, from a lively green to white-gold. In the gaps between the hills, you could see the blue smudges of mountains deeper in the

Carpathians. Even the air smelled as if it had descended from some superior plane, perfumed with the freshest grass.

In the months after my grandmother died, I had started having dreams about Staryava. In the dreams, I was incorporeal but had the ability to fly. My disembodied perception would swoop over the hills of the village, whose skies were always dark gray, on the verge of storm. I felt a strong sense of foreboding in the dreams. It was almost as if I were haunting the village, a ghost myself.

I'm sure part of my preoccupation with my grandmother after her death was that I wanted to hold on to her memory. But I also wanted to fill the silences that I had been unwilling to disturb while she was alive, to start to answer the questions I had felt in her presence for as long as I could remember.

Stefa had gamely agreed to play the role of research sidekick but took no pains to hide her skepticism. "The only way you'll be able to find these stories is in the archives," she had told me that morning as we waited in a cloud of exhaust on the shoulder of a bustling main street in a provincial Ukrainian town near Staryava. Vasyl was in a small grocery store, buying some chocolate and liquor to give to the relatives we would see that day. "In the archives," she repeated in a singsong voice. I bristled and looked across the parking lot.

As much as her comments irritated me, I had to be grateful for how much she was doing for me. Here she was, well into her seventies, tolerating the bumpy, winding trip to the village, an excursion that few relished. Here she was, listing family members we could meet, wondering what we might ask them, weighing whether it would be appropriate to give them cognac or bon-bons or the hand-me-downs I had brought with me from America.

Once we reached Staryava, Vasyl pulled into a green near an old cottage. Stefa and I opened our car doors and stepped into the grass, its thick stalks pricking our ankles. Vasyl waved out the window as we passed; I heard the click of the driver's seat lurching back. He was content to remain in the car alone with his thoughts while we visited, exhibiting the Ukrainian tolerance for open-ended waits that never ceased to amaze me as an American.

As Stefa and I walked toward the cottage, we could make out the thin, clear evidence of the village at work — cows and roosters making their predictable noises; the sharp crack of a farmer thrusting his axe through a log; a stream rippling nearby. The wood siding of the cottage looked old and weary, as gray as a donkey's hide. Nearby stood an array of ancient sheds and barns as well as towers of hay held in place by a rickety pagoda. The cottage was the home of the youngest sister of my late great-grandfather Mykhailo, a woman I knew as Aunt Nastka.

A kindly, buoyant widow approaching ninety, Nastka had been born a few years after my grandmother but technically was her aunt. They had grown up together in Staryava. Nastka had once explained to me that, as kids, she and my grandmother "ate from the same plate."

Stefa knocked on the loose door of the cottage and stepped inside. "Hello?" she called. We hadn't phoned ahead because Stefa didn't want Nastka to get anxious about hosting guests. It would be un-Ukrainian not to have a full spread to welcome visitors.

We heard the shuffle of footsteps. A short, kerchiefed figure emerged from the dark corridor and embraced Stefa. Each woman patted the other's face affectionately and murmured expressions of surprise.

"Do you know who this is?" Stefa asked, gently breaking from Nastka's grasp. I stepped forward; it had been a few years since I had visited.

Nastka's face brightened. "Anna's granddaughter," she said.

With my hand in hers, she ushered us inside and pulled out a chair at a table for me. Then she went over to her small stove to start water for tea.

Nastka's husband had died in recent years, and she lived alone on their farm, making ends meet with a pension south of $100 a month. One of her sons brought her to live with him deeper in the Carpathian Mountains in the winter, but when the snow melted and the green of the hills unfurled, she came back to Staryava. Nastka's house was cozy, the walls colored a bright, cheery blue. We settled in a room near the kitchen, where a rug was tacked to one of the walls, along with a faded print of Jesus at the Last Supper. A delicate border near the ceiling had been stenciled unevenly by hand.

Nastka had beautiful eyes the color of robins' eggs, and they sparkled for a moment with mischievousness. She popped open a vodka bottle and moved to fill the shot glass resting on the table near my elbow, but I stuck my hand over it. The day was young. She gave me a quizzical look but put the bottle down.

The steam from the tea swirled around us as we did some catching up, and I enlisted Aunt Nastka in helping me get our family tree straight. It was head-spinning work: Figuring out how I was related to most of my Ukrainian extended family felt like doing complicated math in my head. An elderly man I had met was, it turned out, my grandmother's cousin; I shared a great-great-grandfather with a dark-haired, heavyset woman with two gold front teeth; a stooped, ancient woman was my great-grandmother's sister. And on, and on.

To make matters more confusing, Ukrainians often refer to cousins simply as "brothers" or "sisters." Only upon clarification can you understand whether a relative is a "native" (i.e., real) brother or sister, or a "second" or "third" one—cousins of different degrees. I liked the sentiment behind the convention, but it tangled the relationships all the more. `

Add to that the fact that, in times past at least, it was an honor to name a child after a beloved relative, even if a close relative of the same generation had already done so. That made our family tree a mishmash of Rozalias and Stepans and Ivans and Annas and Lidas and Olhas. The practice had even extended to me. My middle name, Stephanie, had been given to me to do homage to Stefa, my aunt. She, in turn, had been named after my grandmother's beloved elder brother, whom my grandmother had referred to as Stefan, the version of *Stepan* that was common in Galicia at the time. Stefan himself had surely been named after either his paternal uncle

Stepan or his grandfather Stepan (or both). God knows how far back the line of Stepans and Stefanias went.

As we talked, sorting through the genealogy, I realized that there was not just a cluster of DNA tying me to these hills; the place's claim on me was literally inscribed in my name.

Part of the reason for my visit was that I wanted to ask Nastka about her father, a man named...Stepan Mazur. It was during the lifetime of this Stepan Mazur that the medieval ways of the countryside started to yield to modernity, stirring up the political and cultural conflicts that served as the backdrop of my grandmother's earliest years.

Stefa was right: There was a lot I could learn from the archives. I had submitted a flurry of inquiries to local archives and documents had begun to trickle in. Even basic requests required careful scrutiny; there was another village called Staryava about forty miles north of my family's in Lviv Oblast, and it was easy to confuse the two. As I integrated it all, a world started to emerge.

Stepan Mazur, Nastka's father and my great-great-grandfather, was born in Staryava in 1870. In his mid-twenties, Stepan married nineteen-year-old Anastasia Hul, also of Staryava. Shortly afterward, they started a family. They had seven children, including my great-grandfather, Mykhailo. Their second eldest, he was born in 1898.

The world Stepan and Anastasia's children entered was hardscrabble and bleak. At the time, Staryava fell within the Austro-Hungarian Empire as part of the Kingdom of Galicia and Lodomeria, a lavish name for what was a derided backwater. When we speak of Ukraine today, we think of it being populated by two ethnic groups: Ukrainians and Russians. Galicia, which was the precursor to a large swath of today's western Ukraine, was home to few Russians. Poles, Jews, and Ukrainians were the largest ethnic groups, though they may not have described themselves that way. Many peasants defined themselves by language or religion rather than nationality into the twentieth century.

Galicians who lived in cities tended to be Polish and Jewish. The peasantry was Ukrainian and Polish, though Jews were also present in smaller numbers in the countryside. In the eastern part of the province, Ukrainians were especially numerous. With a population of about twelve hundred, Staryava was about 80 percent Ukrainian; the remaining 20 percent was Polish and Jewish.

Serfdom had ended just a few decades before Stepan's birth, and the peasants of the region, including my great-great-grandparents, were struggling with both the oppressive remnants of the old order and the new order's demands. Life was a complex, grinding ordeal, largely because serfdom had kept the peasants of Galicia in penurious misery for centuries. A system of the kind seems to have been in place as far back as the late fourteenth century, the era of Staryava's founding, which was also the time when the Kingdom of Poland seized the lands of medieval Galicia from the dynasty ruling Kyivan-Rus, an early Slavic state.

Under the Polish crown, serfdom had its first sustained and organized manifestation. Power was concentrated in the hands of the Polish nobility, and the peasants were essentially their chattel, even those who were ethnically Polish. Serfs were bound to a section of land on the estate of a royal or noble, and obligated to work on his behalf up to six days a week. They plowed the fields, brought in the harvest, threshed the grain, prepared the fodder for the animals, and built and repaired roads and the village church. On top of spinning and weaving for the manor, women cooked, cleaned, washed the family's clothing, tended to their children, and cared for the chickens, pigs, and, if the family was lucky enough, horses. If these labors weren't enough, serfs also paid taxes to the manor and state, which were usually provided in kind, in the form of poultry or grain.

The serf had no rights under Polish law, and a landowner could kill his serfs without repercussion. Other forms of abuse were less drastic but more common. "No excuse as to the pressing needs at home was of any use," said a memoirist writing in the early twentieth century, recalling serfdom in a village in central Galicia in the years before its demise. "If one did not appear as ordered, at once the overseer would come.... The lord of the manor was the owner of everything. His was both land and water, yes even the wind."

The fate of the peasants improved nominally under the Austro-Hungarian Empire, which acquired Galicia at the end of the eighteenth century as part of the first partition of Poland. Shortly thereafter, the man appointed to serve as the Austrian governor of Galicia, Count Johann Baptist Anton von Pergen, was dispatched to report on the new jurisdiction. Pergen's impressions were far from glowing; he was particularly appalled by the state of the Ukrainian peasantry. "Since anything the peasant saves only excites the greed of the lord or his official, he naturally seeks to conceal or to consume it," he wrote. "Accustomed to frequent inhumane beatings for petty matters he reacts only to the threat of a raised cane." Ukrainians were "impoverished, poorly housed, poorly clothed, given to drunkenness, lazy, and indifferent." The sum was "more an animal than a human existence."

The emperor, Joseph II, extended some protections to serfs and limited the number of days they were obligated to labor on behalf of the landlord. Joseph was celebrated for this, and it would not have been uncommon to see a portrait of him hanging in a place of honor in the typical Ukrainian hut of the time, much as Lenin would be venerated two centuries later. The peasants despised their Polish landlords but had a childlike reverence for the changing cast of Austrian emperors. Like some righteous grandfather, the emperor would be able to correct the ills against them, the peasants believed. After Joseph's reign ended, some of his reforms were rolled back. Serfdom persisted, and a sense of defeat permeated Ukrainian culture.

In 1848, in response to the revolutionary fervor sweeping through Europe, the Austro-Hungarian Empire abolished serfdom. For the Ukrainian peasantry, that translated fairly quickly into improvements in political status. Ukrainians were permitted representation in the Austrian parliament. The first Ukrainian-language newspaper was published in Lviv. The idea of a Ukrainian nation began to take hold. But improvements to the grinding life of the Galician peasant were few, in part because the ignorance in which their masters had kept the peasants during serfdom made them slow to comprehend their new rights. Perhaps most detrimentally, they were suspicious of the notion of owning property. "Am I to live forever, that I should buy land outright!" went one saying from the time.

It didn't help that the nobles fought the changes tooth and nail. Peasants were ordered to compensate their former overseers for the loss of their services, a burden they shouldered for fifty years after the formal end of serfdom. In 1902, nearly half of all Galician peasant households were still earning their livelihood by working someone else's land.

Slowly, inexorably, the world of the Galician peasant started to broaden. Compulsory education was instituted, spurring literacy and introducing printed literature to what had been a predominantly oral culture. In 1842, only 15 percent of school-age children in Galicia attended school. By 1913, that proportion had skyrocketed to 82 percent. During this time, railroads linked eastern Galicia to the capitals of Central and Western Europe; a railway station was constructed in Staryava in 1864. Cheap factory goods flooded the cities and small towns of the province.

The novelty and expediency of these items made them attractive to peasants, and centuries-old traditions and practices, such as spinning, weaving, processing wool, and wood carving began to decline. Ready-to-wear fashions replaced the homespun linen, wool, and sheepskin that had been the basis of the peasant wardrobe. Metal slowly supplanted thatch as the roofing of the typical Ukrainian hut, and glass became available to fill its windows. Rice, white flour, coffee, tea, pepper, and other spices were added to a cuisine whose original staples had been bland root vegetables and wild fruits, vodka, bacon if one was lucky, and the humble yet sacred loaf of bread. (The Ukrainian reverence for bread continues. A few years ago, I observed my cousin Ihor bag up a few leftover slices of bread and deposit them on a communal windowsill near the mailboxes at his bourgeois apartment tower in Kyiv for one of his neighbors to claim. "Today Ukrainians will throw away a lot of things," he explained. "But still never bread.")

The fortunes of eastern Galicia were briefly boosted by an unlikely source: the petroleum industry. Crude oil had long been a feature of life in the region, appearing as a sheen on puddles or holes in the earth. Men who couldn't make a living as merchants or farmers gathered it by swishing a braid of hay in an oil-laden ditch, squeezing the oil from the braid, then thickening it with clay or manure to sell as fertilizer at the market. The Industrial Revolution set in motion a much bigger demand for oil, and a regional headquarters coalesced around Drohobych, a medium-sized town in the southeast corner of what is now Lviv Oblast. An oil belt extended northwest from Drohobych, and Staryava sat in the center of it. In 1897, a large multinational petroleum company purchased exploration rights in an area that included Staryava.

The petroleum industry enjoyed some initial success. In 1909, the Austro-Hungarian Empire was the fourth-largest producer of crude oil in the world. The peasants of Galicia, however, did not see much benefit from this "black gold." The jobs the industry produced for unskilled workers were dangerous, toxic, and minimally regulated. Oil fields were susceptible to fires and explosions. The industry declined swiftly, bedeviled by a poor transportation system, quickly depleted sources, crude recovery equipment, and war. By the time my grandmother was a girl, in the late 1920s, the oil industry was an afterthought in the Galician economy. In the Polish Business Directory of 1929, three mills, two timber recovery businesses, one quarry, and one gravel transport outfit are recorded as operating in Staryava. There is no hint of the petroleum industry.

While the developments of the late nineteenth century diversified the kinds of food Ukrainians ate and the clothes they wore, these changes did not translate into a wholesale improvement in living standards. In fact, eastern Galicia remained abjectly poor. The area was known as "Golicja i Glodomeria" (with goly and glodny being Polish for "naked" and "hungry"), a play on Galicia and Lodomeria. The most desperate time was usually the fast that led up to Easter, when the cache of potatoes and sauerkraut that sustained families through the lengthy winters began to run out. Those who did not die of starvation were "frail like straw," wrote one nineteenth century Galician memoirist.

An obvious explanation for this state of affairs was that the agricultural practices of the peasantry were stuck in the Middle Ages, literally — an economic historian of the period observed that the scythes, sickles, and other tools used by Galician farmers in 1850 were "exactly the same as those used in the 13th century." Every year, the average agricultural yield in Galicia was the lowest in all the provinces of the Austrian Empire. Add to this the fact that the farms in eastern Galicia had developed in a patchwork fashion, so that a family would have five or six fields scattered throughout the village, and it could take hours just to get to and from them. This inefficient practice continued even into my grandmother's time. "Sometimes the potatoes were close to the house, so we didn't have to carry them far," she told me once. But sometimes the potatoes would be planted on a field far from their house. "If we had to carry them from the forest, we would try to borrow a wooden cart because we didn't have one. If no one lent a cart to us, then we had to carry the potatoes on our shoulders. I carried so many potatoes on my shoulders." A sack could weigh as much as 150 pounds. "You had to carry it with someone else and then you could barely walk."

The labor necessary to sustain such an arduous lifestyle contributed to Galicia's other chief problem: overpopulation. In 1843, on the cusp of the abolition of serfdom, Galicia had a population of 4.5 million. By World War I, it had exploded to more than 8 million — and this growth at a time when emigration was becoming a popular option for escaping the penury of the Galician countryside. Around the turn of the century, about half of Galician farming households were supporting themselves on holdings of two hectares or less — not even close the five hectares a small family needed to subsist. The average couple had seven children. Many, of course, had more.

Peasants considered children a blessing, but they were also an economic asset, a way to expand the labor pool available to work the fields. When these children became adults and married, it was common to divide the land their parents owned equally among them — if, of course, the parents had been lucky and wise enough to own land. By the early twentieth century, intermarriage among landowning families had created class divisions within the peasantry. Even so, would-be farmers could expect little from the plots that resulted when a property was divided into ten or eleven sections. There were jobs to be had in Staryava's sawmill and quarry, but the labor was arduous and poorly paid, even for the Ukrainians who formally pledged allegiance to the Polish state so they could get easier jobs.

This was the dilemma my great-great-grandparents Anastasia and Stepan Mazur faced: an expanding brood coupled with paltry means to support them. So Stepan made a decision that was increasingly popular in Galicia: He signed up to work in the United States.

The opportunity was new. The dire economic realities of Galicia had propelled its peasantry beyond its borders in search of work for years, but only in the mid-1800s did those desperate or brave enough elect to make the long trip across the Atlantic Ocean. Migrants usually stayed just a few years, and could make as many five trips in a lifetime. According to my family's recollections, Stepan also made multiple trips to the United States, probably all to the coal mines of Pennsylvania.

Before I began to study my family's history, I thought of their immigration to the United States as a single moment, an irrevocable jump from "there" to "here." There was the myth of Ellis Island: You broke upon the shores of America and you were here. Who would go back? Many people did.

Stepan's choice transformed the family's prospects. By the time my grandmother was a child, in the late 1920s, Stepan's travels earned him the honorifics *dobriy hospodar*, a title reserved for the most prosperous peasants of the village's landowning peasants, and an *Amerikanets,* an American, for the wealth he earned in his time abroad. For all their worldliness, such men tended to retain a peasant's perspective on life. Usually illiterate and conservative, they preferred that children work the fields rather than pursue an education. And their prosperous status was truly relative. The men might have fields, but they were still farmers, subject to the whims of nature and the market.

Hunger and poverty hounded the Mazurs well into my grandmother's time. She told me that as children she and her older brother would crowd around their grandfather Stepan and wait eagerly for him to give something to them, *skirki* — I didn't know what the word meant. "*Skirki* — you mean like candies?" I asked.

No, I was told. Not candies.

By that time, Stepan Mazur was toothless. He would eat the soft inside of bread and give the children the *skirki*...the crusts!

"Crusts, yes," my grandmother confirmed. "He would give a crust to one of us and then one to the other, depending on how many pieces of bread he ate," she said. "We were so happy when he gave them to us. We liked them a lot."

Looked at in another light, Stepan's choice had seminal consequences. By residing in the United States, even just temporarily, he cracked open a door to the outer world that would never be closed. Stepan left Staryava to acquire the means that would allow him to stay. And he succeeded. From her cottage, Nastka had a view of the fields her father had purchased more than a century before from the proceeds of his trips to America.

Some of Stepan's descendants would see the same value in leaving. But for them, coming back would not be as straightforward.

Aunt Nastka was the youngest of Stepan Mazur's children, and the only one still living. I tried to think about what I could ask her that would illuminate Stepan Mazur for me. I started very simply.

"What did your father look like?" I asked.

"He was tall, like Ivan," she said, referring to my grandmother's younger brother, who had been dashing in his youth. "He looked a lot like him." Then she veered into a story from her youth. Her father had died when she was nine years old, she told us. When he was on his deathbed, she had overheard him say that for her older brothers, his death would be endurable, but for her, his youngest daughter, "it would be a shame." She started to cry a little. She confessed that at the time she had prayed that she would die rather than her father. She was just a useless child, only good for moving the cows around and delivering milk and bread to the laboring adults. What could she really do to help the family?

Nastka's mother died a year later, leaving Nastka an orphan at age ten. Nastka had little to say about her mother and I let it go, not wanting to push.

"Do you have any pictures of your parents?" I asked.

"Child, from where? Where would they have had photos taken?" she responded mildly, her gaze faraway and weepy.

A few moments passed, and then I had a thought. "Who do you get your eyes from, Aunt Nastka?"

"They're from my father," she said. With that, she smiled and squeezed my arm.

4

In Motion

Aunt Nastka's floral house coat was ringing. She fumbled at her breast, retrieving a mobile phone from the front pocket of her top. "*Allo*," she said in the customary Ukrainian way, in which an opening hello is a statement, not a question.

The caller was her daughter Maria, who lived in Italy. Maria had been abroad almost ten years. The last time I recalled seeing her was shortly before she left, at an impromptu farewell party for me she hosted in 2005 at her old apartment, her round face flushed with the joy of company and a few shots of *horilka*, Ukrainian vodka. When Nastka handed over the phone, Maria greeted me with easygoing warmth, as if it had been only a few weeks since we'd last spoken.

We exchanged pleasantries and wondered at the passage of time. I asked her how she liked Italy. "It's fine," she said, her ambivalence obvious. "But I'd like to come back to Ukraine."

Maria was just one of millions of Ukrainians who had left the country in the hard years following the collapse of the Soviet Union, adding to an already sizable Ukrainian diaspora produced by more than a century of poverty and war.

In the 2010s, the period of my visit to Aunt Nastka, Kyiv was considered one of the few places in the country where you could reliably land a job that could comfortably cover a family's housing and living expenses. Elsewhere, the going was tough. Each time I came to Ukraine, I got word of another relative or family acquaintance who had left: A distant cousin had taken a construction job in Poland; a beloved hairdresser had departed for the United States; a former colleague had started working in a restaurant kitchen in the Czech Republic. "Everyone who can leave, has," one of my relatives told me. This didn't account for his own presence in Ukraine, but, then, I knew he had relatives abroad who helped him pay the bills.

Most of the improvements I saw outside Kyiv seemed to be fueled by such steadily flowing remittances. Indoor plumbing. Home additions. Satellite television. Ukrainians were grateful to enjoy some of the comforts that were taken for granted in the West, though frustrated that it was hard to acquire them through a job in their own country.

Phenomenon born of the rapid globalization of the late 20th century, migrant labor and remittances seemed a modern solution to poverty. But from my family's story, I knew these practices dated back much further.

My great-great grandfather Stepan Mazur's achievements may have won a certain stability for his young family, but they offered no respite to his sons and daughters when they came of age. Stepan fathered eleven children in total, and even his holdings—sizable only in a relative sense—would be pitiably small when divided among all of them when he died, as was the custom. With twentieth century farming practices in Galicia barely progressed beyond medieval times, Stepan's children faced exactly the same problem their father had: They had no ways to adequately support their families.

My great-grandfather Mykhailo was one of the first of Stepan's children to confront this quandary. In 1922, at the age of twenty-four, he had married a striking young woman from Lopushnitsa, a village just west of Staryava. Rozalia Prokopiak was stunningly beautiful, with high cheekbones, full lips, and crystalline eyes that she described as gray in her official documents. The eldest child of Ukrainian farmers and four years younger than Mykhailo, she was straightforward and confident, and is said to have taught her new husband to read. She was so self-possessed that her younger sister used the formal *vy* when addressing her.

Per tradition, Rozalia came to live with Mykhailo at his father's house in Staryava. It must have been crowded, as Mykhailo's set of brothers and sisters was still growing. Mykhailo's mother, Anastasia, had died a few years before, and his father, Stepan, still in his early forties at the time, had remarried, taking as his second wife a fellow villager named Tatiana.

In 1923, when Mykhailo and Rozalia welcomed their own first child, they called him Stefan. This name was probably an homage to Stepan and might have even been spelled that way when the child was born, but the family referred to him using the version of the name common in Galicia at the time. My grandmother was born two years after Stefan and named after her mother's sister, Anna.

A third and final child was born three years later and was named for Mykhailo's brother Ivan, who would have been on Mykhailo and Rozalia's minds that year. Just two years older than Mykhailo, he had taken their father's cue and left the family when he was seventeen to work in the United States. Eventually, he ended up in Cleveland, where low-skilled jobs were plentiful at the time. But unlike their father, Ivan elected to stay. In 1928, the year Mykhailo and Rozalia named their third child after Ivan, his petition for naturalization was granted and he became a U.S. citizen.

Ivan's new status meant that he could invite other family members to join him. Letters must have crisscrossed the Atlantic to that effect. My theory is that my grandmother's youngest brother got his name out of a revived closeness that came from the excitement of Mykhailo possibly joining his brother in the United States.

The rationale fits. Rozalia and Mykhailo yearned for a house of their own. Stepan and Tatiana had four children together (including Aunt Nastka), which, with Mykhailo and Rozalia's three, meant that a simple four-room Ukrainian hut had to accommodate at least seven children, not to mention a number of adults. As it had for his father, work abroad would give Mykhailo the ability to earn more money in a few years than most Ukrainian farmers would earn in a lifetime. It would mean not just a house, but fields to farm — fields that could possibly sustain his family for generations.

Leaving would have its costs, however. Rozalia would be alone to tend to their small children. Even if Mykhailo would be gone just a few years, they might not remember him when he came back. My great-grandparents must have fretted about how his absence would shape their young family, what they all would lose.

Mykhailo would also be leaving the community he had been a part of his whole life. He was the founding treasurer of the village's branch of Prosvita ("Enlightenment"), a club that promoted the Ukrainian language and the idea of a Ukrainian state. It was one of the most important organizations in the Ukrainian national movement following the demise of serfdom. In Staryava, the club staged concerts, celebrations, and dramatic productions and operated a small library of Ukrainian-language titles.

Among my grandmother's belongings, I found an old photograph that seemed important — it had been nicely mounted, as if it had once been framed and hung on a wall. In the image, men and women are lined up in rows. The men are wearing suits and ties. The women are dressed in traditional Ukrainian garb: blouses with flowery embroidery running along the sleeves, dark red vests that come down to the thigh, light aprons with fringe at the bottom, layers of beaded necklaces. In keeping with the fashion of the 1920s, their hair does not fall below the chin. A woman kneeling in the center of the group wears a sash that says "Staryava." Ukrainian script on the back of the mount identifies the group as Staryava's Prosvita.

As I studied the photograph, I realized that there was something strange about it. A couple of the figures didn't quite fit: A man in the second row had a head double the size of anyone else's. A man on the far right was curiously small and had feet that hovered unconvincingly over the grass. Slowly I recognized his pointy chin and light brown hair. The man was my great-grandfather. The photograph had been doctored to include him and others using some kind of 1920s version of Adobe Photoshop.

The circumstances of the photo's construction are lost to time, but the care and affection that prompted it translate clearly. By going to America, Mykhailo was leaving a community of which he was a treasured part.

By October 1929, the decision had been made: Mykhailo would go to the United States. He couldn't have known then — no one knew — that the prosperous America he anticipated was about to begin a decade-long plunge into an economic depression of unprecedented scale. The photo in the passport that was issued to him that month shows Mykhailo as a slim-faced man with a trim mustache and confidence in his eyes. On October 29, he was in Warsaw, receiving a visa to immigrate to the United States. By November 11, he was in London. Just one week later, the SS Leviathan brought him into New York Harbor. He was thirty-one years old.

It's hard to know whether the financial crash that fateful autumn would have given Mykhailo any pause. Even if the news did penetrate his universe, I'm not sure that the U.S. stock market collapse would have held any meaning for him, a Ukrainian farmer barely literate in his own language, to say nothing of English. Even if he felt some concern, if he had some inkling of the extended calamity that was coming, he would have been an outlier. At the time, the severity of the crisis was far from obvious. On November 18, the day Mykhailo arrived in the United States, the *New York Times* led with news of a Federal Reserve Board report that showed that, despite the unprecedented stock market dive the previous month, wages in both the industrial and agricultural sectors were holding strong.

The hardship would become apparent with time. As Mykhailo traveled to Cleveland to meet his brother Ivan, his plan was finally in motion. By being in the United States, he was that much closer to going back to Staryava, to being able to give his family the life he wanted them to have. But it wouldn't be a year or two before he returned to Staryava. Not even five. More than thirty years would elapse before Mykhailo would see any members of the family that he left behind – and some he would never see again, including his eldest son, Stefan.

The sky over Cleveland is typically gray, the lake a muddy blue, the grass stiff and yellow in the winter and pillowy and green in the summer. From the bridges that stretch over the Cuyahoga River, you can see freight yards and immense ships moored along the docks waiting for cargo to be loaded into their holds. When you wade into Lake Erie, dark pieces of algae lap against your calves and sharp rocks push up into the soles of your feet. Modest homes with neat yards bump up against each other in neighborhoods formed by immigrants seeking communities of their own.

When I close my eyes and think of my hometown, the elements that come to mind are not that much different from what my great-grandfather encountered when he arrived in Cleveland from Staryava almost a century ago, in 1929.

Mykhailo and I shared a few years on this earth. When I was born, he was living in a nursing home receiving round-the-clock care. A massive stroke two years earlier had left him partially paralyzed and unable to speak clearly, but it didn't stamp out his love of company. My parents and I visited him, my mother carrying me on her hip; he could still play pinochle with his one good arm.

He died in 1985, when I was three years old. I don't remember him, but every so often I see him in members of my family – and myself. My grandmother inherited his strong jaw. In photographs where he is huddled among friends, I can feel his garrulousness, a trait shared by my aunt Olga. Comments from my mother suggest that I bake with his spirit, not caring that I spill flour on the flour or leave buttery fingerprints on the faucet. In America, Mykhailo worked as a baker, and was known for his gusto and exuberance.

The traces of the people who came before us are everywhere, even when we can't see them.

Mykhailo reunited with his elder brother in Cleveland in the last months of 1929. By then, Ivan had Anglicized his name to John and made his home on the Southside, a rough neighborhood west of the Flats, where Cleveland's heavy industry was located. The proximity to the low-skill jobs in the city's steel mills, coal yards, and foundries made the Southside a prime destination for newly arrived immigrants. By the second decade of the twentieth century, refugees from the collapsed Austro-Hungarian Empire had displaced in number and influence the Irish who had settled the Southside almost a century earlier. Poles and Ukrainians were most heavily represented in the mix, along with Slovaks, Russians, and smaller numbers of Greeks, Germans, and other nationalities.

The Southside was an American melting pot if there ever was one, but one in which the ingredients retained their constituent parts. New arrivals normally associated with members of their own ethnic group—and, more narrowly, those who belonged to the same parish. The modest streets of the Southside were (and still are) jeweled with churches, none more stunning than St. Theodosius, a Russian Orthodox cathedral with a profusion of green domes that sits on a bluff overlooking the Flats. Immigrants from the Carpathian Mountains had started the church at the turn of the twentieth century, electing to follow the Moscow Orthodox patriarchate rather than the Pope. John, too, had abandoned the Greek Catholic tradition he had been raised in and joined St. Vladimir's, a Ukrainian Eastern Orthodox congregation that had formed in the Southside in 1924.

Mykhailo, who went by Mike in the United States, probably had little time to contemplate the intricacies of the switch; the cacophony of American life was on him in full. First there was the task of getting reacquainted with John, who was starting to enjoy some good fortune following a long spell of tragedy. After a few years in the United States, John had married a woman he had grown up with in Staryava. Her name was Katherine, and she had made her way through Ellis Island about six months before he did. They welcomed their first child, a girl named Josephine, in November 1919, but she died at the age of four months. In 1927, Katherine, just thirty-two, herself died after years of suffering from kidney disease, leaving John a single father to their six-year-old daughter, Annie. John had, however, happily remarried, and his second wife, a young woman of Ukrainian extraction named Helen, would soon give birth to a son.

The culture of the Southside was a hybrid of the Old World and the new. In the summer, men in horse-drawn carriages canvassed the Southside, hawking bags of nuts and recently-picked peaches. Immigrants of all extractions converged on the brick concourse of the West Side Market, on West Twenty-Fifth Street, where fresh produce was cheap and you could get your hands on a whole goose or chicken. Some residents of the Southside built smokehouses in their picket-fenced back yards and smoked the birds, saving the feathers for pillows or duvets as they had in Europe. The smoke would lift into the gray Cleveland sky, where, when the wind blew a certain way, it would mix with the coal smoke from the freight yards, the reek of rotting flesh from the slaughterhouses, the exhaust of the tar and asphalt plants, and the gas emitted by the oil refineries, all of it mildly earthened by the Cuyahoga River. It was a smell like nothing else in the world, and for many it was the smell of prosperity and freedom.

In the most important ways, Mike landed on his feet. The 1930 census would show him employed at a bakery — perhaps the same bakery where John was working as a truck driver. By June 1930, Mike had the $200 he needed to open a bank account. His command of English was so poor that he reported neither written nor oral skills in the language, but his brother had both. Mike was getting by, saving money and sending it to Staryava. It was working, his plan. The house in Staryava was becoming more than a dream. Reality was in his favor.

Back in Staryava, his family waited.

While my mom and I were sorting through my grandmother's things, I found a photo of my grandmother as a child. The image startled me. I assumed that we didn't have any photos from Staryava because my family was not able to take anything with them when they were exiled to Siberia. But a number of photos did survive. They probably had been sent to Mike in the years before the war.

The photo, of Rozalia with her kids, sister, and brother-in-law, was probably taken shortly after Mike left in 1929, because the youngest child, a plump Ivan whose bangs are brushed flat against his forehead, doesn't look to be older than two. Rozalia wears her hair bluntly cut just below the ear, like a New York City flapper, and my grandmother, then about four years old, has her hair styled the same way and is wearing a necklace of white beads, which is the companion of the necklace belonging to Anna, the aunt she was named after, who stands directly behind her. Perhaps at some point that day the elder Anna leaned over, gave her young niece a smile, and pointed out to her that their necklaces, like their names, matched.

The photo clearly marks a special occasion. Anna's husband is dressed in a suit and tie; there is a kerchief in his breast pocket. As dashing as he looks, his strong fingers, darkened at the tips, betray him as a farmer. The children's outfits are from the same seamstress. Little Ivan is dressed in a white smock with thin dark lines that ran from hem to collar. The same cloth forms the crisp collars that protruded from Stefan's jacket. The belt that cinched at Stefan's waist has the same square white buckle as the belt running around my young grandmother's dress.

Their ensembles could not have been cheap. My grandmother said that her mother thought Mykhailo was "raking in money with a shovel in America." Maybe the outfits and the photo had been paid for in a burst of optimism, in the belief that Mykhailo's sojourn would mean that the family could regularly enjoy such niceties. Maybe Rozalia was regretting the photo for its expense even as it was being taken, and in a fit of anxiety snapped and yelled. For a culture known for producing grim family portraits, Rozalia fixes the camera with a gaze that seems particularly stony, and Stefan and Anna look especially unhappy: each of Stefan's little hands is clenched in a fist. Maybe Rozalia yelled with ferocity, called the kids stupid, and told them to give her some peace. When my grandmother grew up and got frustrated, she would do the same thing with my mom and Olga, and the anger seemed reflexive, as if it sprang from behavior that had been inherited so long ago that she did not even question it.

Whatever the reason for the photo, any optimism or hope for the future held by the family was misplaced. It was 1930, and the photograph seems to catch the Mazur family echoing the aches and troubles of their world.

Rozalia does not appear to have gathered the family for another portrait in Staryava.

By the mid-1930s, despite an economy mired in depression, Mike seemed to hit his stride. He liked baking. It involved working with his hands, just as farming had, and he did it well. St. Vladimir's became a proper parish in 1933, opening a church about a mile down the street from the Mazur house in Tremont. Just as in Staryava, Mike made the church the center of his life outside work. He frequented the Ukrainian National Home, a former mansion on West Fourteenth Street that the Ukrainian community used for concerts, art exhibits, lectures, and other cultural events. Mike's bakery was a union shop; he found meaning in union life and was an active member of the Teamsters.

He took such a shine to America that it was decided that Rozalia and the kids should join him, that the family should live in America permanently. In 1935, he filed a declaration of intention to apply for citizenship. But the timing — oh, the timing — was bad. It was clear that the employment situation was dire, that even Mike's good fortune was precarious. About forty-one of every hundred men on the Southside couldn't find a job in 1934. The Southside watched the hulking factories of the Flats nervously. For a community whose livelihood depended on industry, the vile emissions of the factories were a welcome sign of health. When work in the factories slowed, everyone suffered. "The smokestacks were just empty tubes sticking into the sky," a memoirist of the Southside of the Depression era related with dismay. "No black smoke, no white smoke, no red, yellow, or orange smoke."

John had left his truck-driving gig, and when Prohibition was repealed, in 1933, he opened a tavern next door to his house. It didn't do very well. According to the 1940 census, Mike was making the most money in the Mazur household, having earned a respectable $1,560 in 1939 for his thirty-five hours a week as a baker, slightly more than the average annual wage in the United States. John's wife, Helen, brought in $1,040 from her work as a meringue maker at a pie business, while John reported just $640 in income from the bar. John and Helen had one child in their care — John Jr. His daughter with his late wife Katherine, Annie, had headed West and at age seventeen married a man in Butte, Montana.

Within a few years of his departure, Mike had made good on his intention to finance a house for his family in Staryava. But as soon as it was standing, it began causing problems. By that point, the financial desperation afflicting the United States had spread around the world. Rozalia had trouble keeping up with the payments on their dream house.

Debt was a common predicament in eastern Galicia. It largely unfolded along ethnic lines, with Ukrainians and, less frequently, Poles, the debtors, and Jews the lenders, offering rates that were often usurious. This arrangement had its origins in feudalism. Not allowed to own land under the Habsburgs, Jews had become middlemen between the Polish nobles and the Ukrainian and Polish peasantry, serving as landlords, small moneylenders, and tavern keepers. In 1868, the Austro-Hungarian Empire loosened longstanding regulations on usury, and interest rates skyrocketed. Peasants could pay as much as 522 percent interest on a loan.

Sixty years later, when Rozalia was raising her children, the Austro-Hungarian Empire was gone; Galicia was now part of the Second Polish Republic. But exploitative lending persisted. Unlike many women, Rozalia didn't have to deal with a drunk husband or father-in-law who drained the family's coffers. Yet she was still providing for three small children on her own—and even with the money coming from Mike, she struggled to make ends meet. "My mother didn't take on debt for improvements; we just spent money on food," my grandmother remembered. "She went to the Jews often. She was taking on a lot of debt and signing for it but when the time came to pay, she didn't have the money. I don't even want to remember that."

Despite Mike's best efforts, Rozalia and her children led lives filled with hunger, hardship, and arduous physical labor, like generations before them. In need of even the basics, the Mazurs periodically walked the perimeters of Jewish homes to see if the inhabitants had discarded any cookware because they had violated kosher law.

From an early age, my grandmother and her brothers worked hard helping their mother around the house and on their land. "Children weren't doted on like they are here. No one would carry a five-year-old around. From five to seven o'clock in the morning, you guarded the cows," my grandmother recalled.

> You would run to school by eight o'clock and you would not even have time to wash your feet. You stayed in school until one p.m., then you came back home. You ate something; maybe you would do a few lessons. At three o'clock, you had to watch the cows again because in the morning they had come back too quickly. If you were studying, you would take a book with you and study there. While you were reading, a cow would run off, and you would have to run after it, and [make it] turn back to where it should be. As soon as you opened the book, a second cow would be off.

If there was not enough food, the cow wouldn't listen. It would go where there was food. If it saw rye or wheat, it would try to eat the wheat and rye. If the cow ate wheat, then the rye wouldn't grow and we would be in trouble. We were beaten for that. We were beaten for not stopping the cow. The cow was so stupid. It did not want to go to where it was supposed to go.

During the summer, it was hot and on Sunday you would guard the cows and at nine you had to go to church. At half past eight, you came back home with the cows. I would maybe brush my hair or wash my feet and run to the church. At three o'clock in the afternoon, you would look after the cows again. They would be being bitten by flies. The flies would bite and the cow would put her tail up and run away very quickly. You would run after the cow. You would lose it, you would call for it, you would worry about it. Then you would come back home and be beaten for losing the cow.

One of my grandmother's cousins who grew up in Staryava guarded his family's horses at night. "I would sleep on the horse," he told me. "If I got a bad mark at school, my father would beat me with a stick. Why did he beat me? How could I study on a horse at night?"

After completing sixth grade, at most, the children became full-time laborers, helping tend the family's fields scattered throughout the village. At times their crops failed, and they would be so desperate that they would steal grass from the neighbors so that their livestock wouldn't starve. At least once, the Mazurs faced the serious possibility that they would lose their home.

Rozalia paid her loans in kind with whatever the family could spare. "Here, go give these to Yankel," she would tell my young grandmother, handing her a batch of freshly-laid eggs tied up in a handkerchief. The little girl would march to the homes of Staryava's Jews or the bigger community in Khyriv, almost five miles away, to make another small dent in the family's debt.

"I would never wish that life on you or your children or your grandchildren," my grandmother told me once.

An ocean away, Mike Mazur was enjoying a very different fortune. On March 18, 1938, he became an U.S. citizen. He would never master the intricacies of the English language, but he took great pride in his status. From there on out, he voted in every election and always for the Democratic Party, in keeping with his union loyalty.

He usually dressed in a suit and tie before heading to the polls, befitting a practice he considered a privilege.

He looked forward to introducing his family to the country he had come to prize. The family in Staryava began to prepare to immigrate. But Mike wanted to wait until times were a bit better, when there were jobs to speak of and desperation didn't crackle in the air. So they waited, thinking that a better time would surely come. What they got instead, in September 1939, was something far different from what they had hoped.

5
War

To some Ukrainian peasants, preoccupied with the harvest and other matters of survival, the prospect of war seemed far off. Usually at least one person in a village could afford a short-wave radio, and those who had them could pick up the rumblings of conflict.

Nazi Germany had developed an insatiable appetite for territory, raising alarm throughout Europe. In the second half of the 1930s, Germany annexed the Rhineland, Austria, the Sudetenland, then all of Czechoslovakia. In 1938, it grew fixated on reacquiring Danzig, an independent city-state over which Poland enjoyed some jurisdiction. Britain and France rallied in solidarity and presented a unified front: Disturbing Poland's territorial claims was a line Germany was not to cross.

Many Ukrainians shrugged off these troubling developments. Others wondered how a war could rework politics in their favor. Ukrainians strongly resented Polish rule, which had been in place since the end of World War I, when Galicia had fallen into Polish hands. Among the terms of the peace negotiated with Germany following World War I was that Poland would safeguard the rights of its minorities. In reality, the protection existed only on paper – specifically, the pages of the Polish Minority Treaty, which was signed in June 1919 by representatives of Poland and the Allies, shortly after the completion of the Treaty of Versailles.

Under the Second Polish Republic, the list of Ukrainian grievances against the Poles, already lengthy, grew even longer. The Polish government ensured that Ukrainians remained a subservient class by barring them from jobs in education, transportation, law, and taxation, and excluding them from various parts of the military. It closed university Ukrainian-language departments and mandated the teaching of Polish in Ukrainian schools.

These repressions reinforced a growing desire for Ukrainian independence. The concept had started to gain steam in the late nineteenth century, as ethnic minorities throughout Europe experienced improved education and living standards and began to yearn for the privileges enjoyed by the ethnic groups running the states that governed them. Ukrainians' wish was briefly granted with the establishment of the Western Ukrainian People's Republic in eastern Galicia in 1918. Within a year, though, Poland had occupied the fledgling state, effectively shutting it down.

Some Ukrainians began to see violence as the best response to their predicament. A radical faction of Ukrainian nationalists perpetrated several acts of terrorism to draw attention to the independence fight and protest Poles' treatment of Ukrainians; their most notable attack was the assassination of the Polish minister of the interior in 1934. The Poles eventually retaliated with a brutal show of force against Ukrainian communities, further hardening their state's largest minority against them.

As tensions rose in the late 1930s, the Germans played to Ukrainians' hopes. Anton Hrycyszyn, a Ukrainian born in eastern Galicia in 1921, recalled that "the Nazis began beaming to us from Vienna in Ukrainian and we nicknamed Hitler *vuiko* [uncle] as he promised to 'liberate' us and grant Ukraine independence." It didn't turn out that way. On September 1, 1939, the day the Germans invaded Poland and World War II began, Ukrainians' dream of German-supported sovereignty met grim reality. The Germans dropped small, delayed-action bombs throughout the countryside, and attacked Dobromil and Khyriv, the towns closest to Staryava, on September 12.

The area only stayed in German hands a few days. On September 17, the Soviet Union invaded Poland from the east. An agreement between Hitler and Stalin, the Molotov-Ribbentrop Pact, divided Polish territory between the two powers. The Soviets claimed most of eastern Galicia, including Staryava, for its Ukrainian Soviet Socialist Republic, meaningfully linking what is now western and eastern Ukraine for the first time in hundreds of years.

The revolving door of occupiers was a spectacle to the peasants. Peter Potichniy, a villager from eastern Galicia who was nine years old in 1939, observed that the Germans were well groomed but that the "Soviet troops were an awful sight, badly dressed with torn shoes and boots, dirty and smelling" on the account of "some kind of tar-based powder that was sprinkled on the soldiers' uniforms to prevent lice infestation." A Staryava resident remembered Soviet soldiers smoking loose tobacco rolled in errant strips of newspaper. Another recalled someone handing a bouquet of dahlias to a Soviet soldier to welcome him, only for the soldier to throw them to the ground in disgust. "What we need is bread," the soldier said.

Initially, the Soviets and Germans presided over their new conquests as partners and allies. In the fall of 1939, their mission complete for now, the Germans considered what to do with the expanded labor pool suddenly at their fingertips. Germany had a strong tradition of foreign workers before the war, particularly in agriculture. While Nazi dogma frowned on the prospect of tainting the German empire with foreign blood, the promise proved so enticing that they decided to allow a sizable — but manageable — cohort of foreign workers into the Reich. In mid-November 1939, Nazi leader Hermann Göring directed labor administration authorities "to conscript civilian workers, in particular Polish girls, on a large scale." He wrote, "Their utilization and in particular the wages they are paid must be such as to place productive workers at the disposal of German firms as cheaply as possible."

Even though Staryava was technically in Soviet hands, the German border was less than fifty miles away. The Germans widely advertised that labor opportunities were available in the Reich. Word made its way even to Soviet-occupied territory. A pittance to a German worker could be a fortune to a struggling Ukrainian farmer. Leaving was not preferred, but starving was much worse. Some Ukrainians decided to take the Germans up on the offer, including Stefan, my grandmother's older brother.

"Stefan? Oh, Stefan!"

During one of my visits to Staryava in the 2000s, I was walking through the village with Ivan, my grandmother's younger brother. A woman we encountered had recognized Ivan even though decades had passed since he had lived in the village, and called out to him. The woman was tickled to run into Ivan. She was so petite that when she embraced him, the top of the babushka tied firmly around her head did not even brush his chin. As they traded updates, I noticed that whenever she got especially excited, she pushed her fist against Ivan's chest.

Somehow the subject of Stefan, my grandmother's long-dead brother, came up. The woman beamed at the mention of his name. Stefan had been so handsome, so smart, so upstanding, so well dressed. So tall! The woman punched Ivan lightly on the chest as she named each of these attributes.

Listening to her, watching her, I felt the exuberance that powered her gestures. My grandmother had described Stefan in similar terms — but I was stunned to hear him brought to life by someone outside my family. Stunned to witness that he wasn't just a myth, that he had once been a real person.

Stefan's significance to my grandmother had been evident to me since childhood. In her house, she had, of course, prominently displayed her photo of him as a young man. Gratitude rang out in her voice when she spoke about the ways in which he had stuck up for her while they were growing up. She had named her first daughter Stefania after him. My tall, self-assured younger brother Alex brought him to mind, she liked to tell us with pride. She spoke with no such emotion about anyone else. My grandmother had been married three times, but it seemed to me that Stefan had been the most important man in her life.

That was clear even in her last decade, when she went to great lengths to honor his memory. Part of the family lore about Stefan was that he had joined the nationalists to fight for Ukraine's independence during the war. He had been killed in battle, most likely by the Soviets, who by that point had become the nationalists' primary enemy in the region around Staryava. His immediate family members — among them my grandmother, Rozalia, and Ivan — had been exiled to Siberia as punishment. In Siberia, the Mazurs had heard from a woman who claimed to have been near Stefan's bunker at the time of a Soviet ambush; presumably he had been killed then. But official confirmation of where, when, and how Stefan died — all of that was missing, and it troubled my grandmother for decades.

The collapse of the Soviet Union made it possible to imagine that some of these details might finally be unearthed. Nationalism surged in some parts of Ukraine after the end of Soviet rule, and the people who had borne arms in the name of Ukrainian independence throughout history were celebrated in a manner that had been denied under the Soviets. An effort began to recover and give proper burials to those who had died in the name of the nationalist cause half a century earlier.

My grandmother waited for years to see if any of the roving grave searchers could locate Stefan's remains. Eventually they concluded that they could not. My grandmother was bereft. "He is gone," she told me once. His name had been listed in a book about Ukrainian nationalists, "but what is that to me? I thought, 'If I don't find him, I must put up a monument for him. I must.'"

So she asked Stefa to go to Staryava and arrange for a monument for Stefan to be built next to the gravestone of their grandparents, Stepan and Anastasia Mazur. Stepan Mazur had been a generous patron of the village church, and their resting place is on the edge of the hill where the church sits, with a beautiful view of the village.

"My brother is now close to my grandfather and grandmother. Well, he is not there, but the monument for him is," my grandmother said. "On the monument — I wanted it put a little bit differently, but I wasn't present — they wrote *Stefan Mazur*, around the date when he was killed, and they engraved his picture. The monument is also dedicated to all the people who gave their lives for the freedom of Ukraine. I did it. I said that while I'm alive I will do it. I think it cost around $4,000."

"Four thousand dollars?" I gawped. This was a woman who balked at spending four dollars on a pint of strawberries.

"Yes, yes. Don't look at me," she said. "It cost money. They made it and then brought it and put it there and I am happy. He has a monument there. He is gone."

Stefan was gone—but who had he been? As I sought to stay close to my grandmother, I found myself coming back again and again to the elder brother she seemed to have loved more than anyone else.

I knew that he had been born in 1923, two years before my grandmother. Like her, he completed six years of school at most. Ukrainians were the least educated of the ethnicities in rural Galicia, though some of the most promising students could, if their families mustered the funds, attend a gymnasium for Ukrainians in the nearby towns of Drohobych, or Striy or, in the rarest of cases, Lviv. Such a possibility was not in play for the Mazurs. They had no choice but to take a decidedly material view of status: Fields owned trumped books read.

Stefan's early life, like my grandmother's, was filled with work. As soon as he could speak in sentences, his father expected him to feed the pigs and geese. Soon thereafter he was sent to shadow the family's precious cow. As he got older, if the family's fields were worn to dust, he may have looked both ways before running to a neighbor's fields and gathering as much grass as he could in a blanket he had grabbed from the stable, brought it to the cow, and watched with satisfaction and some guilt as she ate. Like my grandmother, he would have dug up hundreds of potatoes in the fall and gathered them in heavy sacks that he carried on his back. With his father in the United States from the time he was six, he probably watched, with increasing weariness and a premature sense of responsibility, as the stash of potatoes in the cellar grew smaller as the winter wore on. Perhaps, they would sometimes dwindle to nothing, and the flesh across his stomach would tighten and tension would fill him as he awaited the early light and rushing water of spring.

A camp for Ukrainian youth was set amid the spruce forests of Staryava. Participants could take in the crisp Carpathian air and play in the cool waters of the Stryazh River. But it was a camp for a small and entirely different class of Ukrainians from the one the Mazur kids were part of. One camp counselor remembered barefoot children from the village who were Anna and Stefan's age stopping their chores and watching the young interlopers with suspicion. The notion of children organized for the sole purpose of leisure was foreign to them.

The one outlet the Mazur children had was Prosvita, the Ukrainian cultural club Mykhailo had help establish in Staryava before he left for the United States. By 1929, the club had a building of its own in the village and it was close to the Mazur farm. In his few breaks from field work, Stefan may have borrowed Ukrainian-language children's books from the club and participated in the theatrical productions it staged with the village kids as players. The club promulgated a vision of Ukrainian patriotism that was inflected with righteousness. "We wanted to be highly moral, nationally conscious, and religiously observant," one of Stefan's contemporaries in Staryava said about their youth. Perhaps Rozalia sent Stefan to Prosvita to maintain a connection to the spirit of his father. She couldn't have known that by doing so she was also pushing him toward a certain fate.

As a brother, then, Stefan would have watched over his younger siblings. They would have huddled together for warmth while sleeping. Eaten from the same plate. Lain together on the flat, warm expanse of their house's kiln, and listened as their elders reviewed the merits of the latest theatrical production staged by Prosvita, or criticized the recent decision of the sawmill director, or debated the wisdom of erecting a cross in front of the school, as a local Ukrainian had done, only for the Polish authorities to knock it down and tear up the blue-and yellow wreath that had been hung on it.

When the antics of Stefan and his siblings put the adults at their wits' end, the children would be shooed outdoors, and they would have each other for entertainment. Maybe they made swords out of sticks and tried to fence with each other, or chased each other in the thick grass that pricked at their ankles. Maybe they were joined by their numerous Mazur cousins. Maybe a classmate. Only Ukrainian classmates, though, because though they knew Poles and Jews from school, where they all studied together without much ado, the adults kept them apart otherwise, urging them to socialize only with *nashi* — ours.

In 1948, in the immediate aftermath of World War II, the Allied powers set up the International Tracing Service, which housed information about the millions who were killed, arrested, or displaced during the war. If you were looking for someone, you would write to the ITS, and it would consult the more than 190 million documents in its possession relating to the war in Europe. Months, if not years, later the ITS would tell you what it had found. Only relatively recently, in 2007, did the ITS grant access to its vast holdings to the public, signifying its shift from a tool for reuniting families to one serving a primarily historical function. The U.S. Holocaust Memorial Museum, in Washington, D.C., is one of the few places in the world where you can bypass the records request process and query the database yourself.

For a while, I lived about a mile's walk from the Holocaust Museum, and I started spending afternoons at one of the ITS terminals, trying to see what I could find about my family, about Stefan. His story kept pulling at me. He had come to represent a glaring hole in my understanding of my family, a hole I increasingly sensed needed to be filled.

The ITS delivered. I discovered that by December 1939, two months into the war, Stefan was en route to Germany as part of a contingent of six men from Staryava. The archive held a lime-green registration card Stefan had filed during his time in Braunschweig, Germany, a town of 250,000 between Berlin and Hannover that was a regional industrial center. My grandmother had said that Stefan had misrepresented his age to qualify for work, and here was the proof: The card listed his birth year as 1920, not 1923. He was sixteen, pretending to be nineteen.

Stefan was by far the youngest of the group of six Staryava men. Unless the others lied on their forms, the man closest to him in age was Andriy Kril, who was twenty-four. Stefan was likely the charge of his twenty-seven-year-old uncle, Mykhailo's brother Josef, who was also part of the group, as were three men who had served in various leadership capacities in Staryava's Prosvita. Here was a hint of Stefan's character, I thought. He was considered mature enough by the other, older men to make the trip. I saw from other documents that some of these men had brothers who were the same age as Stefan. They did not go. Stefan did.

The group registered at the Arge labor camp in Braunschweig on December 2, 1939. The *Braunschweiger Tageszeitung*, the local Nazi organ, had written glowingly about the camp's opening that July, reporting that the "neat barracks had grown from the earth... at the edge of pulsating fields." A postcard used to recruit laborers shows the camp as a picture of order, with stable-like wooden cabins set apart by bright cement sidewalks. Braunschweig's medieval town center is a smudge on the horizon. In addition to its proximity to "pulsating fields," the Arge labor camp boasted running water four hours a day and regular sanitary inspections.

By the spring of 1940, more than half of the fifteen hundred men living in the Arge labor camp had come, like Stefan, from occupied Poland. Italians, Serbs, and Greeks were also present, along with a small group of Germans who stayed a few days a week. The men were housed according to their nationality. Country of origin had no bearing on whether the workers were subject to a curfew, however; at 9 p.m., the front gate that surrounded the complex was locked for all.

The men from Staryava were in Germany at the invitation of the German construction giant Philipp Holzmann AG, which had received a commission to build a railway yard in Braunschweig for train cars to be sorted. The men were likely disappointed, if not dismayed, at what they found upon their arrival. The labor conditions for foreign workers — voluntary or forced — were abysmal. The hours were punishing, the clothing and equipment run-down or insufficient. Already low wages were reduced for all manner of reasons. Many of the people Stefan likely labored aside also had one foot in childhood. One wartime Braunschweig resident recalled Ukrainians as young as fourteen toiling in the city. It is perhaps indicative of how his first assignment worked out that after about nine months, Stefan was in the employ of a different company, Schilling.

The Germans enacted strict laws to keep foreign laborers apart from the general population. The measures that governed residents of occupied Poland were "pure harassment and denigration," wrote one German scholar in a book about foreign workers in the Reich. The laws barred former Polish nationals from using public transportation and fraternizing with German women. They were not able to enter German bars or restaurants or attend German cultural or religious events. They had to wear a badge and were subject to a curfew. They could in some cases be tended to by a German barber, but only if special equipment was used. All of this was complicated by the fact that nationality, ethnicity, and war had colluded to make the easy assignation of individuals to groups almost impossible. Piecemeal invasions and multiethnic populations resulted in seven different categories of Poles in the German system, each theoretically subject to a slightly different set of rules once they came to work in the Reich.

If there was a universal to be found among the foreign workers' experience in Germany, it was that the conditions were often far less comfortable than advertised. In the Arge barracks where the men from Staryava first lodged, illness was rampant. I can only guess that this might be the reason why, within five months of arriving in Braunschweig, Stefan was registered at an apartment building in the city, and then, an indeterminate amount of time later, at yet a different one.

Word spread quickly in the occupied territories of the difficulties migrant workers had to endure in Germany. By the spring of 1940, the Germans found they could no longer entice all the able-bodied men they needed to willingly migrate for work. The "population had fallen victim to an anxiety psychosis" at the prospect of moving to Germany, complained one Nazi official charged with overseeing labor deportations. In April of that year, the Germans changed their approach. They implemented compulsory labor drafts for men between the ages of fifteen and twenty-five (women were also conscripted), and authorized coercion when targets resisted deportation. Nazi officials gave local village leaders quotas and tasked them with drawing up lists of people from their community to send west.

In the beginning, these leaders often tried to be systematic in their selections. The first to be sent off were often people on the fringes of village society, or young men and women who came from families with many children. As the war continued and the quotas remained, the selections became less discriminating and more harried. People could be grabbed off the street and sent west. The only people who might be able to keep you safe were kin with positions of influence in the German administration.

Between 1939 and June 1944, more than one million people from Nazi-occupied Poland were sent to work in Germany. Conscripts from central and eastern Ukraine that before the war had been under Soviet, not Polish, jurisdiction, were subject to particularly brutal conditions. These laborers, known as *ostarbeiter* ("eastern workers") were consigned to a lower rung in the Reich's social scheme than workers from what had been Poland. The *ostarbeiters* were expected to subsist on the measly rations allocated to prisoners of war, and the fences that enclosed their labor camps were topped with barbed wire. After the war, more than sixty-four hundred German companies, including Phillip Holzmann, admitted holding workers against their will in deplorable conditions and contributed to a multibillion-dollar fund to compensate former *ostarbeiters* and others who had been forced laborers.

During the early years of the war, though, the environment wasn't that bad. When Stefan was in Braunschweig, Ukrainian laborers from occupied Poland were accorded more respect under German rule; they were, after all, a lynchpin in the Germans' strategy for Eastern Europe. They were given home leave. They could write to their families. They didn't always have to wear a badge. A Ukrainian aid organization operated throughout Germany. While conditions that many Europeans found themselves in during the war hardened them irrevocably against Germany, the men from Staryava may have found that their time in the Reich had an opposite effect. They may have come to admire the way the Germans ran things—how clean the sidewalks were, how reliable the running water, how orderly the governance. It's possible that they thought that what Ukraine needed was to be more like Germany. It's possible that they thought that what they needed was to be more like the Germans.

According to the registration cards, by the spring of 1942 almost all of men from Staryava had left Germany, perhaps to bring that vision home.

The photo of her brother that my grandmother displayed in her home is from Stefan's time in Germany. When I was a kid, Stefan had seemed to me confident, wise. Now, as an adult, I see the youth in his face. I imagine him within the dirt-streaked walls of the Arge labor camp, where tattered sheets covered the windows and men drank beer and sang late into the night. I wonder at the courage it must have taken to leave his home for the first time, and the responsibility to provide that he must have felt to make that choice so young. Yet I also see his Aryan features, his carefully swept-back hair, the sharp lines of his suit. While much about his stay in Germany remains unknown, what that time did to this boy's mind is the greater mystery.

Back in Soviet-occupied Staryava, a repressive calm prevailed. The Mazur family was desperately focused on making ends meet under the Soviets. The Ukrainians of eastern Galicia welcomed the new regime with varying degrees of trepidation. Most were happy to be independent of Poland. Those who had communist sympathies — a significant minority, mainly in the cities — were thrilled. For Jews, too, the Soviet regime offered some improvements, as anti-Semitism was officially outlawed (though in practice often still observed).

The Soviets quickly made good on various promises: Ukrainian-language schools and newspapers were reopened; Ukrainian studies was reintroduced as an academic discipline at the national university in Lviv. In Staryava, the Polish teachers at the school were replaced with Russian ones who seemed to harbor less prejudice toward their non-Polish pupils. The Polish teachers "would not give us the right marks even if we wrote the assignments with our feet, not just our hands," one Staryava native remembered. "I have a report card from the Poles and one the next year from the Russians. Under Russia, I received grades of 'excellent' — all 5, 5, 5. But under Poland, everything was 3, 4. A 5 was not given."

The Mazurs, however, were among the many Ukrainian families who were suspicious. They had heard accounts of the famine that ravaged the peasantry in Soviet Ukraine in the early 1930s. Almost four million Ukrainians died of starvation after the Soviets imposed wholesale collectivization of agriculture. Peasants had been forced to give up even the grains they hid in their shoes. How could that be? And even from the beginning the Soviet army and government seemed chaotic and bumbling. The towns of eastern Poland were not Paris, but the men of the Red Army seemed elated to taste the exotic fruits of the West — not exactly a vote of confidence for life in Soviet Russia. One Red Army soldier in Soviet-occupied Lviv "was seen outside a hosiery shop wearing women's bras over his ears for earmuffs; another standing in the middle of the street, tried to blow one up, looking it over with incredulity," reported the historian Jan Gross. A Soviet lieutenant arrested for drunkenness in Lviv told a fellow inmate he would accept another prison sentence if it meant the opportunity to spend more time in the West.

The Soviets' record in rural places was mixed, at best. They sought to increase literacy in the villages, especially among women. Compulsory meetings were organized to teach peasants the principles of communism. In 1940, a branch of Komsomol, the Communist organization for youth, was formed in Staryava. But the meetings could be long and nonsensical to the point of farce. The Red Army requisitioned farm equipment and food with abandon. In October 1939, when the Soviet regime held its first election in its newly conquered territory, it employed extensive propaganda. "There are millions of factories, cars, field guns, tractors, tanks, and six hundred sixty-five thousand combine harvesters. Soviet workers are masters, they go every year for vacation to health spas," the Communist Party claimed in the material it circulated in eastern Galicia before the election. "They retire at 65 and it is not true that when aged they are used for soap."

Within months, the utopian character of these promises was revealed to be false. The educational system was in upheaval. School curricula were suffused with Soviet propaganda. Censorship proliferated. Churches came under attack. Collectivization loomed. The Soviets outfitted the stores they took over with barrels of cheap liquor, exacerbating the already prevalent compulsion to drink. "Get people drunk and you could do what you want with them," one Staryava resident remembered. "Make them a member of the Party, make them stupid. And all of the sex—all done while drunk." Most troubling were the arrests and deportations of civilians, which could occur without warning or reason. Before long, it was clear that "everyone lived, ate, and dressed worse than before," noted a Ukrainian from the region.

My grandmother had completed school the year before the Soviets invaded. As a fourteen-year-old, she devoted all of her time to working the fields. With Stefan in Braunschweig, Rozalia must have especially needed her help. My grandmother's immediate future seemed clear—she would move between the blistering work of the fields and the solemn confines of the church. At some point, however, this equation was interrupted. Her life would soon be indelibly changed.

6
Womanly Silence

Of all the people I encountered in my search through the past, my grandmother's first husband was the most deeply shrouded in mystery. His existence was undeniable, for without him my aunt Stefa, his only child, would not exist. But my grandmother had shrugged off Stefa's queries when she asked about him. Once, she told Stefa that if her father had survived they would have likely lived better. But materially? Emotionally? Stefa hadn't asked for clarification.

We knew a few things: We knew he had been an ethnic Ukrainian, and we knew his name was Yosip Punko. Stefa had used her father's surname before she married. Under Soviet rule, per Russian custom, she was addressed by her first name and patronymic — *Stefa Yosipivna*, daughter of Yosip — at school or in any formal context. Every day, then, would have contained echoes of him.

We knew, too, that my grandmother had been very young when she gave birth to Stefa. Once, when I interviewed her, she said she had been eighteen. But she stumbled and paused when answering, as if she needed a moment to recall her age correctly. To this day, I don't know if she misinformed me deliberately.

A detail: One of my grandmother's cousins remembered Yosip Punko as a joker. He was the kind of person who would jump out from behind a wall to scare you and then laugh.

We knew that during the war, Punko, not a Jew but an ethnic Ukrainian, had been apprehended by the Nazis for some infraction, and that he had died in a concentration camp. Stefa was just a baby at the time, too young to remember anything.

And we had a photo. One photo. It had been in Stefa's possession for so long that she couldn't remember who gave it to her, or who told her that the women flanking her father were his aunts. But when I looked at the photo, I instantly noticed the relation between Stefa and the boy. He was about sixteen, and had a widow's peak poking out from his wavy black hair. Stefa was the only person of the older generation of our family who had hair that dark; everyone else's ran the gradient from sandy brown to blonde. The same was true for the boy's dark eyes, which stare at the viewer directly—eyes that, on Stefa's face, shimmered. His lips were thin and long, like his daughter's. Over his tie and suit jacket, he wore another jacket, a thick one adorned with what looked like military pins and ribbons. The additional layer of clothing made him look more filled out, and older than his years. But when you looked at his face, there was no doubt about it, you saw a child.

As it turned out, we possessed one other thing about Yosip: rumors. After my grandmother died, my mother, Aunt Olga, and I spent hours methodically sorting through my grandmother's belongings at her house in Cleveland, deciding in bursts of conversation whether an item should be saved, sent to Stefa in Ukraine, or earmarked for Goodwill. We moved from closets to heavy-drawered bureaus to the well-stocked refrigerator, sorting through sweaters, winter coats, soft linens, Ukrainian books, photographs, and plastic-wrapped loaves of frozen bread that looked like bricks.

As we sat on my grandmother's soft couches, with the afternoon light fading, the edge of the rug upturned and the room's framed seascape askew in a way my grandmother would have never allowed, Olga recalled a story she had heard a long time ago. According to this tale, Yosip Punko had first become involved with my family not through a relationship with my grandmother, whom he eventually married, but through an affair he carried on with *her* mother, Rozalia Mazur. Of course, as Rozalia was married to my great-grandfather, Mykhailo, her affair with Yosip Punko would have been unsustainable. The rumor was that she encouraged Yosip to marry her only daughter, my grandmother, instead. The story was astonishing...but not impossible. By the time the war started, Mykhailo had been away in the United States for ten years. Rozalia was only thirty-seven. Stefan, her older son, was working in Germany and his brother Ivan was not even a teenager. My grandmother would have had no ally in the house to help her resist marriage to Punko.

My mother, at least, thought the story was plausible. Rozalia had favored Ivan, whereas she could be curt and dismissive with my grandmother. Was that lack of favor enough of a hint that you could offer your daughter in marriage to your former lover?

Who told Olga the story? She couldn't remember.

At one of the ITS terminals at the Holocaust Museum back in Washington, I typed in the words *Yosip Punko*. The database spit back a list of entries. I clicked through a few of them. Then I opened one that showed me a bronze-colored envelope with Punko's name, the letters as perfectly composed as if they had been written by a first-grade teacher. Only the spelling of Yosip had changed — to the German *Josef*. Yosip was now "Josef Punko."

The envelope contained Punko's file from KL Mauthausen, a Nazi concentration camp north of Vienna. A librarian at the museum translated the essential bits for me: Punko had died of "gastroenteritis" at 4 a.m. on July 13, 1942. Three days later his body was cremated. He had survived in the camp for little more than a month, having arrived on June 6. The file also contained pages of administrative questions in typed German, questions about the deceased's money and valuables. I was not surprised that the spaces next to these questions were blank.

On the fourth and last page, however, one question had been answered. In the space near "next of kin," the librarian informed me, was my grandmother's name. "Anna geb. Mazur:" Anna née Mazur.

Tears pricked the corner of my eyes as I heard this. My grandmother had been seventeen at the time—and already both a mother and a widow.

When Punko died in the summer of 1942, Staryava looked different than it had even one year earlier. Most notably, it was now under German control, not Soviet. In late June 1941, Germany had reneged on the Molotov-Ribbentrop Pact and invaded its former ally, the Soviet Union, as part of Operation Barbarossa, sparking a dramatic escalation of the war. The Germans had Moscow in their sights—they wanted the nerve center of the Soviet Union for their empire. Just a few miles from the border with Germany, Staryava was one of the first villages to see Nazi troops come in.

Many Ukrainians in eastern Galicia welcomed the change in regime, had even been hoping for it. A Nazi official recalled the enthusiasm with which the Ukrainians of Dobromil, the biggest town close to Staryava, greeted the Germans at a rally that June:

> The crowd of many thousands, festively dressed...presented a lovely, colorful picture. Every time the name "Adolf Hitler" was heard, the crowd roared with enthusiasm and clapped. During all of my trips in these days, my car was buried in flowers in every town. When one stopped somewhere to ask directions, one was immediately surrounded by hundreds of applauding people, ready to help.

By then, most Ukrainians in eastern Galicia who were not communists had come to strongly oppose the Soviets. In the first days of the German occupation, their resentment had reason to mount: As the Red Army retreated in the face of the German onslaught, the Soviets massacred the men languishing in the prisons under their control, many of whom were supporters of the Ukrainian nationalist movement. In Dobromil, several hundred Ukrainian prisoners were discovered dead; in Lviv, more than three thousand prisoners were killed. All in all, the Soviets are thought to have murdered at least ten thousand prisoners as they fled Nazi forces.

Many local Ukrainians erupted with fury against the Jews. They tended to associate them with Soviet power due to the perception that they were disproportionately represented in Soviet government ranks, an impression the Germans played up to murderous ends as they installed themselves in the region. Certain Ukrainian nationalists, eager to earn the Nazis' favor, had no problem arresting and murdering Jews; it aligned with their agenda of cleansing their land of "hostile elements." In Lviv, crowds led by Ukrainian militiamen killed hundreds of Jews on the city's central streets. In Dobromil, a synagogue was set on fire. "In the first hours after the Bolshevik withdrawal, the Ukrainian population displayed commendable activity against the Jews," read one satisfied German field report.

The violence represented a boiling-over of prejudices that had long simmered in the region. Under feudalism, the Ukrainians, Jews, and Poles of eastern Galicia had been "trapped in a vicious circle of self-interest and survival," wrote one scholar. Even when the yoke of serfdom lifted, relations remained strained. Ukrainian anti-Semitism was fueled by the belief that Jews had a significantly greater share of the wealth. "The Jews here exploit the poor people terribly, and everything goes well for them," a Ukrainian living near Staryava complained to a Ukrainian newspaper in the late nineteenth century.

In truth, the Jews of eastern Galicia were also very poor. People of all ethnicities who worked as blacksmiths, window makers, and other kinds of artisans — many of whom were Jews — had been left reeling in the wake of industrialization. In eastern Galicia in the early 20th century, the number of merchants — a traditionally Jewish occupation — vastly exceeded the number of merchants in wealthier parts of the Austro-Hungarian Empire, despite the fact that their clientele had far less money to spend. The profit of the typical Jewish merchant was "barely enough to provide for Sabbath bread and candles," wrote one historian. Ignoring these subtleties, Ukrainians also faulted Jews for their prominent role in the liquor trade. While Jewish culture frowned upon drinking, drunkenness was rife among Ukrainians, particularly men.

The longstanding tension between Jews, Poles, and Ukrainians instilled in all three cultures a casual bigotry that held even in the best of circumstances. Ukrainians had some ghastly proverbs: "From infancy, a Jew has his own bazaar within." "Don't consider a Jew a human being or a goat or a cow." Jews, for their part, portrayed Ukrainians as primitive, uneducated, and prone to alcoholism. The Poles disdained both groups. "There were good people," acknowledged a Jewish man named Herman Teicher, who grew up in a predominantly Ukrainian village close to Staryava and survived the war by hiding in the forests of the Eastern Beskids. "But the majority, especially the young ones, were extremely anti-Semitic. It showed up the first days when the Germans came."

The warm welcome the Ukrainians paid the Germans turned out to be steeped in naiveté. The Germans did extend some help to the Ukrainian cause. They launched more Ukrainian-language schools and permitted Ukrainians to hold low-level positions in municipal governments. While the Germans considered both Poles and Ukrainians to be racially inferior, no question, they gave special dispensation to the Ukrainians of eastern Galicia where the nationalist movement was strong and at first supportive of Nazi power.

For the villages that came under German rule, though, it soon became apparent that the Germans were not going to be benevolent overseers. A representative of the Nazi administration appeared in church on Sunday mornings and gave the worshippers their orders for the week. Ukrainians had to turn in their weapons. Higher taxes than ever were imposed; alcohol production was halted. "Other orders followed in quick succession because, as the Germans put it, *Ordnung muss sein* (orderliness must exist)," one Ukrainian from eastern Galicia remembered. If you didn't follow the commands, the punishment was simple: At best you were arrested and sent to the camps. At worst you were shot.

Peasants were rounded up by the thousands and put to work in factories and on farms in the Reich — not voluntarily, like Stefan, but as forced laborers. Requisitions of grain and livestock intensified.

"We were waiting for the Germans," my grandmother acknowledged. "But they came and they were the same as the Russians. The same." She continued:

> Even when the day was short, you were not allowed to go outside after six o'clock. If you went out, there was a train station [in Staryava], if [a German] saw you, he could shoot you from the train. People ran away and hid in their houses. Kids were allowed outside until nine o'clock, but after nine they were not allowed to go outside. If you heard the train coming, you would think "the Germans are probably coming" — that's what we would tell them — "the Germans are probably [on] there" — and all the kids would run home. If there was a chicken around the house, they would stop, shoot it,

and take the chicken on the train—or a piglet, if they saw one. Pig or calf, they would shoot it and take it on the train.

People hid everything and were afraid for their families. One army left and another arrived. That's all that changed.

The Ukrainian nationalists had aligned themselves closely with the Germans. In a fit of euphoria that descended in the days after the Germans invaded the Soviet Union in June 1941, the leaders of a radical wing of Ukrainian nationalists took to the radio airwaves and proclaimed themselves the leaders of an independent Ukrainian state, administered under the auspices of the Germans. The Nazis did not look kindly upon such overreach. By the fall, many of these nationalists were in camps such as Auschwitz, Belzec, Sachsenhausen. Even so, the nationalist movement nurtured some hope that the Germans would have a change of heart and support Ukrainian self-rule.

The Germans had different plans for Ukraine—and for Ukrainians. They imagined Ukraine's fertile fields as the agricultural engine of a German empire stretching from eastern France to the Urals. The Poles, Ukrainians, Jews, and other ethnic minorities native to the land were not to benefit from this vision. Before Germany invaded, the Nazi leadership had prepared an elaborate plan to expunge them through mass murder, deportation to Siberia, and enslavement.

The hard going on the eastern front in the years that followed Operation Barbarossa meant that the Germans never implemented the plan, known as Generalplan Ost. They did, however, expand to their new territories the restrictive penal framework they had imposed in western Poland. On January 1, 1942, the Nazis adopted a special penal code that made death the standard sentence for virtually all crimes committed by former citizens of the recently conquered territories. The point of the law, wrote the German legal scholar Diemut Majer, "was not the maintenance of order but the deterrence and annihilation" of everyone who wasn't ethnically German.

In the early months of 1942, Yosip Punko's responsibilities and bur-
dens were considerable. His household had been expanded by his
new teenaged wife, my grandmother, as Ukrainian brides typically
moved into the home of their groom. The ability to grow food on
the farm may have spared his family the severe hunger afflicting
the cities, but that wouldn't have inoculated them against the taxes,
the requisitions, and the fear that accompanied German rule.

And then the Nazis took him.

I recorded my grandmother talking about this, so I have her
exact words: The Germans "found a weapon or something and arrested him. They found some ammunition close to the house."

Mauthausen was the deadliest concentration camp in the
Reich in the summer of 1942. The majority of its inmates worked in
the quarry. A colonel in Patton's army who helped liberate the
camp in 1944 described skeletal prisoners weighing as little as
eighty pounds hauling stone half their weight up from the quarry.
If the prisoners faltered, they could be beaten to death on the steps,
their bodies "pushed from the precipice down to the jagged rocks
below."

The Nazis sometimes lied about the cause of death in their records, especially if a prisoner met a violent end. Punko may have
died of a stomach virus at four o'clock in the morning, but he also
might have been executed as he ran toward a barbed-wire fence
trying to escape. Or he may have collapsed carrying a gigantic
block of stone up from the quarry, only to be pushed into the abyss.

Through the ITS, I discovered that Mauthausen wasn't the
only concentration camp in which Punko had been imprisoned.
The Nazis had transferred him to Mauthausen from Auschwitz,
where, in April 1942, he had first been interned for about two
months. He had come to Auschwitz from a prison about 90 miles
away in Tarnow, Poland, a staging point for transfers to Auschwitz.
His arrest likely occurred in the weeks or months after the imposi-
tion of the new penal law in January.

That was as far back as the records on Yosip Punko went.

About the same time that I learned these details of Punko's fate, I
heard from an archive in Poland. It held a spotty collection of vital

records from the church in Staryava. At my request, the archive had emailed me details from the records of dozens of my family members. I read their report in bed one morning, shortly after I woke up. I was pleased to see that the archive had the birth records for my grandmother, her brother Ivan, and Stefa, too. They even had the record of my grandmother's marriage to Punko. How interesting, I thought, to see that they were married in the depths of winter, on February 16, 1941. My grandmother would have been ...fifteen, a week away from her sixteenth birthday. I winced. So young—so much younger than Punko, who I knew from his death certificate would have been twenty-eight at the time of the vows. Was that strange, such a large age difference? I went back to Stefa's birth record, and I realized that the date—August 9, 1941—meant that my fifteen-year-old grandmother would have been about three months pregnant on the day she wed Punko.

Suddenly, I was wide awake.

I was so pleased to make a discovery about my grandmother that, without thinking through my actions, I forwarded the archive's report on to my mom and my aunts Olga and Stefa. In my haste, I didn't consider how Stefa might feel to learn that she had been conceived outside of marriage, at a time when my grandmother was so young.

Her response, which I received in an email, was simple: She appreciated knowing the information. Her birth date had long been the subject of some confusion, she reported. Throughout her life, she had marked the day in July and counted her years back from 1942. But Ivan had told her at some point—again, the details had fallen away—that she was actually born in August. He had never intimated that it was August of the *previous year*, that she was a year older than she had always believed.

My mom and Olga responded to the news as more proof of how hard their mother's life had been. From there, the response faded into a heavy silence, all of us contemplating the worst but not saying it. All of us contemplating the reality of a fifteen-year-old becoming pregnant by a man almost twice her age.

In prewar eastern Galicia, a thick fog surrounded sexual matters, one generated partly by denial and partly by ignorance. The church exerted a tremendous moral authority in village life, and Christian guidelines on such matters were clear, if a bit vague on the particulars. It was drilled into the young that they were to remain chaste, but who knows what they understood that to mean? The reserve was so great that a girl could obey her parents and not kiss boys but still wind up pregnant because no one had ventured further and explained sex. When my own mother got her period when she was fourteen, she was so in the dark about reproductive biology that she thought she was dying. It is fair to think that girls like my grandmother didn't understand their bodies or the bodies of men, to say nothing of the consequences when the two came together.

Maybe my grandmother's union with Punko was the product of young love, reckless and urgent. But to believe that would be to upend most of what I knew of my grandmother and her life in Staryava. For all the beauty and community of life in Ukraine there was something particularly brutal about it. "I would never wish that life on you or your children or your grandchildren." Her words.

Within nine months of Stefa's birth, Punko was in Auschwitz. Three months later he was dead. Whatever he had been to my grandmother — whether he was a rapist or a manipulator or her first love, or somehow something in between — that was dead, too.

Once again, the photos. I spent so much time studying the photo of my grandmother as a child and Punko as a teenager that I eventually noticed that the backdrop of the photo of the young family was the same as that in the photo of the boy and the two women. Yes, in both photos, the trunks of two dark trees occupy the space above the people on the left, and some dark, round clouds, maybe intended to be trees cast further off, encroach from the right. My grandmother was about three in her photo, and Punko, the child in the man's uniform, looked to be about sixteen. The photos were likely taken at the same studio around the same time, as there were thirteen years between my grandmother and her future husband.

Thirteen years can be grasped in many ways. One way is to see two photos, one of a three-year old girl and one of a half boy, half man, and know that just as the girl grows to be as old as the boy — when she is still just half-girl, half-woman, in other words — she will be married to the boy — now a man, no question — and in a matter of months bear him a child.

While going through the paperwork my grandmother had filed away, I came across a small, yellowed prayer booklet. It looked like the kind of thing my grandmother would have received through the church sisterhood, a group of older ladies who regularly met for coffee, sugar cookies, and company in the hall behind St. Vlad's. My grandmother had written her first name along the title page in English letters, but her last name in Cyrillic.

The booklet contained a few prayers in Ukrainian, and then pages where the owner could write the names of people who needed her prayers. One page contained lines for people who needed prayers for their health, and on it I saw the names of my mother, my aunts, and my great-grandparents — all people who presumably were still living at the time.

The next page was for those who had died. The list there was longer: twelve names. Working with the family tree I had put together, I traced my grandmother's relationship to each of the people she had listed and noted it lightly in pencil on the page. Stefan — her brother, obviously. Kateryna — that would have been her father's sister. Anna — another aunt. The one name I couldn't place was "Osip." I left the space next to this name blank.

I continued to flip through the rest of my grandmother's paperwork. To emigrate from the Soviet Union, my grandmother had had to submit a battery of vital records — her birth certificate, proof of immunizations — and she had kept them all. Many of the documents had been reproduced in Siberia as the originals were left behind in Staryava when the family was deported. One of the documents was a death record for Yosip Punko — the date listed was within a week of the one listed in his Mauthausen file. I realized with a start that on that document his name was spelled *Osip*.

The question of what had happened to my grandmother as a young woman continued to haunt me. When I was next in Ukraine, I asked Aunt Nastka how my grandmother met Punko.

Nastka's reluctance to speak was tangible. "Your grand-mother? God, I don't know. I'll tell you, child, what I know. What I don't know, I won't say," Nastka replied.

She stayed quiet, so I pushed a bit. "My grandmother was very young when she married," I said. "Do you remember that?" Nastka would have been about ten at the time.

"Oh, she was so young," she lamented. Silence. Eventually, she said, "She simply got ensnared."

Stefa was with me, of course, and it was she who asked, "By whom?"

"I don't know what happened. Only the one in the sky knows," Nastka hedged.

"You're hiding something," Stefa said suspiciously.

"She got ensnared in something when she was young, and what happened, happened." Nastka's wide blue eyes had the guile-lessness of a child's.

"What, you don't know any of the details?" Stefa asked.

"Who knows?" Nastka was quiet. "Stefa, people said that your father had been spending time with your grandmother and later your mother was put in a situation and given to Punko and that was it. Who knows? The one in the sky knows and will judge," Nastka asserted again.

"God, my mother struggled a lot," Stefa muttered, looking down at her plate.

"Yes, your mother had to go, people said," Nastka continued, looking at Stefa. "She went to live with Punko, and who knows how it was. The heavenly God knows. Her father wasn't there, and she was young. Later, you were the only child of Punko, and that was it." She sniffled a bit, perhaps from emotion.

"Do you know what happened to him?" Stefa asked.

"I will tell you what happened. My sister Ruzia's husband — yes, the one in Poland — your father, and one more man, they...

How do I say it, I don't want to offend—" Nastka looked over at me.

"It doesn't matter anymore," Stefa said.

"It's in the past," Nastka agreed. "They were thieves."

Stefa looked at me and asked, "Do you understand?" I nodded quickly.

"Child, they stole," Nastka continued, unimpeded. "I remember the Germans coming. The Germans came to our house," she said, now addressing Stefa, "for Ruzia's husband, your father, and that other man. They did a roundup of the house, and they took them and left. My brother-in-law's boy was guarding a cow, and he had a bit of gunpowder. They found it. They took them all to Auschwitz." As she spoke, I remembered my grandmother's words: "*They found ammunition or something around the house...*"

That was all that Nastka knew. Except there was one more thing: Nastka informed us that some of Punko's relatives still lived in Staryava, perhaps the daughters of his sister. I saw a small wave of pain wash over Stefa's face. "Why didn't anyone tell me?" she asked. She had never met a relative from her father's family.

Nastka shrugged in innocence.

"Oh, what a comedy," Stefa said, shaking her head.

We decided to call on this relative of Punko's. Nastka felt that the visit warranted a different housecoat, so we left the living room where we had been drinking tea and walked outside to the entrance of the cottage where Nastka slept so that she could change.

After she emerged, the ever-patient Vasyl started the car and we drove slowly along the dirt road that separated the fields from the houses. We pulled up near a simple brown house that had three windows, a tin roof, and a satellite dish that protruded from one side. The car still running, Nastka got out and started walking up the mild slope to the house. I followed. Nastka knocked on the door, but there was silence. We waited a few moments.

"She's not home," Nastka said, waving her hand vaguely toward the house. She turned and head back down the slope. "When you come next time, I'll show you," she said to Stefa, who had been trailing behind us and was still only partly up the slope.

"I don't need to be shown anything. Megan is the one who's interested," Stefa said but Nastka did not seem to register the comment. We got back in the car and started driving slowly toward the center of the village.

"Do you remember the name of Punko's sister?" I asked Nastka, who was gazing calmly out the window.

"Wait, I will try to remember," she said, holding a crooked pointer finger to her lips in concentration.

"He was Yosip," Stefa prodded. "What was her name?"

"I will tell you," Nastka vowed.

She couldn't remember.

"Women are silent," Svetlana Alexievich wrote in her 1988 book, *The Unwomanly Face of War*, which documented Soviet women's experiences in combat during World War II. "They did not believe themselves. A whole war is hidden from us."

I don't know how to account for my grandmother's silence. Maybe it was trauma and shame. Maybe it was heartbreak. Maybe it was the inevitable distance that grows between our younger and older selves. My grandmother sometimes referred to the dissonance she experienced when recalling the vastly different world she had previously inhabited. "I've already forgotten my old life," she told me once. "It's the truth. Even now, sometimes I think, was I there or not?"

Her old life. It was something I could not forget. It had become a part of me, too. The stories about my grandmother that I told myself began to take on the weight of memory; hazy but vivid scenes from my grandmother's life flickered in my mind.

Yosip Punko likely came into the Mazurs' life in the waning days of 1940. By then, the Soviets had been in power for about a year, and the chaos of the early days of their rule had settled into a milder, more quotidian dysfunction. Perhaps Punko had seen Rozalia around the village—beautiful Rozalia, with her crystalline gray eyes—and started stopping by the farm to talk to her. Rozalia thought little of Punko—he was younger than her and a bit of a *durak,* a fool—but she was exhausted. With Mykhailo away in

America for ten years and her two youngest kids at home — her eldest, Stefan, away in Germany — Rozalia's good sense may have been
stretched thin. It was nice to have someone to talk to who wasn't a
child or an in-law. It was nice to talk to a man. Before long, maybe
Rozalia felt herself relying on those talks more than she had bar-
gained for. Maybe, she eventually found herself wanting to do
more than just talk.

In any case, at some point, Punko formed an affinity for her
daughter. At least, that is how the scenario plays out in the stories
I tell myself. Maybe Rozalia spurned Punko's advances or grew
tired of them, and one day, angry and impetuous, Punko came by
when he knew Rozalia was out selling *pirozhki* at the bazaar in Lviv
or negotiating with the Jewish mortgage lenders in Khyriv. On that
day, perhaps he approached the stable where my grandmother was
clearing out manure or the fields where she was watching the cow.
Maybe she concentrated on the wooden wall of the stable or the
blue Galician sky while he pawed at her. By then she had endured
the beatings of childhood; maybe she thought this was just a different kind of beating. Maybe that's what she believed until she felt
the pain of being entered and knew that whatever was happening
to her, whatever it was, it was serious and wrong and it would have
consequences.

Maybe she lived for months with the fear of what would come
of this scary, painful thing, and she kept it deep inside herself because there was nowhere else to keep it. Maybe Stefan could have
helped her, but he was away in Germany. Maybe she didn't understand what those consequences were exactly until her mother observed her throwing up one day and asked her if she still had her
monthly bleeding, and she said no with a look of confusion, and a
cold terror squeezed Rozalia's heart, and she arranged for Punko to
marry her daughter. Because while Rozalia couldn't change the
past and had little power to soften the future, she could help absolve her daughter and grandchild in the eyes of God.

Maybe Rozalia also needed to absolve herself.

In the church birth register, Stefa's surname is recorded as Mazur, not Punko. This was a sign that my grandmother's family held

higher status in her village than her new husband's. Perhaps it was also a sign that Rozalia had authored their union, chosen it for her daughter as the best of a bunch of bad options. The Mazur family knew from bad options.

Maybe.

I would never wish that life on you or your children or your grand-children. My grandmother's words.

Her experience with Punko was embedded in that statement, I believe. Sometimes we do not hear people when they say things to us. Our imaginations fail us; we are not able to grasp what is possible.

I wondered how much else I did not know.

7
Grandfather

My grandmother's marriage to Yosip Punko wasn't the first mystery I encountered in her life. On the topic of my own grandfather — the man my grandmother married after Punko died — she had also been silent.

When I was growing up, as far as I could tell I had no grandfather to claim. At least, not that I knew of. My grandparents on my father's side divorced when my father was young, and my dad's dad had slinked away into obscurity. So I did not find it odd that my mother's father was also missing.

Only as a teenager did I notice a stack of photographs of my mother as a child stashed in a kitchen drawer where we kept our coupons. A balding man with a small port wine spot on his upper forehead was in some of the shots. His eyebrows were always pursed together in a way that conveyed perpetual concern. When I asked about him, my mother explained that the man's name was Andrew and that he was her father. She said this with a look that was puzzled yet detached, so that at first I didn't grasp what she was telling me. Then, I did.

The moment passed quickly, and nothing more was said. But a window had been opened.

One afternoon in the spring of 2003, while I was still in college and planning my first trip to Ukraine to study the language, my mother shared that her father was still alive and resided in a small town near Staryava. She herself had just learned this from Stefa while the two were exchanging details about my trip.

The news was unsettling to both me and my mom. A grandfather — what the hell? By early adulthood, I had only picked up a smattering of details about the man. I had gleaned that he was an alcoholic and that my grandmother had divorced him — acrimoniously — for that reason. That was it.

My mother was uncertain about whether I should visit Andriy, as my grandfather was called in Ukrainian. She said that when
she told my grandmother that I might meet him, she had become
angry and dismissive. Averse to conflict, I didn't raise the prospect
of meeting him with my grandmother before I left. However, once
I arrived in Stefa's place in Truskavets after my language program
was over, the possibility came back to the fore.

Stefa thought I should pay my grandfather a visit. Her opinion
held some sway with me. She wasn't Andriy's biological daughter
but with Punko dead, he had been the only one she had ever
known. Even given Andriy's past behavior, whatever it was, Stefa
felt that that a visit was in order. My curiosity won out. I told Stefa
we should go.

Stefa put out a call through what she termed the *selyanske radio*—the village radio, or gossip mill—and came up with Andriy's
current address. We set out one morning with Ivan, my grandmother's brother, who had been a contemporary of Andriy's in Siberia. Vasyl had to work, so Stefa's son, my cousin Volodya, drove
us from Truskavets.

My grandfather lived in a two-story farmhouse with white
siding and black shutters in a small town about five miles from
Staryava. The house would not have been out of place in a small
town in New England, which was a rare thing to observe about a
dwelling in Ukraine in the early aughts. As we walked toward the
porch, I felt queasy, and stifled an urge to run back to the car.

A round-faced, auburn-haired woman answered Ivan's knock
on the door. She wore a blue velvet nightgown with fake diamonds
sewn along the scoop neck. As I neared the doorstep, her eyes
bounced between Ivan and me and grew wider the more he explained. I gathered that her name was Luba, and she was Andriy's
daughter. She shoved her hands across her bosom when she realized who I was, and continued to look at Ivan with wide eyes. After
a few moments, Luba's gaze slid from Ivan to the sharp-jawed Volodya, who had joined us on the doorstep. "Oh!" she exclaimed in
a fit of modesty, and disappeared into the house.

Ivan, unembarrassed, trailed Luba inside and gestured for us to follow. A blond man emerged from the dark room Luba had run into. He introduced himself as Luba's husband. Andriy was out on a walk, but someone had been sent to find him and bring him home. Luba's husband led us into the cozy living room, and anxiously offered me a chair.

Luba reappeared from her bedroom, still buttoning the last clasps on her pink silk blouse. "Are you Olga's daughter or Nadia's daughter?" she asked as she rushed to bring enough chairs into the room to accommodate us all.

"Nadia's," I answered. *She knew who my mother was.* Luba was younger than my mother, which meant that Andriy must have told her about his other daughters. I had never heard of Luba before that day. Luba stopped and clasped her hands, a smile radiating across her face. Nadia's daughter, from America!

I sat stiffly in the chair and stood up to shake the hands of people as they entered. Anna, Andriy's sister, had a long, square chin, clear skin, and large, wide blue eyes. Luba's son, a dark-haired ten-year old with a heart-shaped face and full lips, was named after his grandfather. The young Andriy was loquacious, and I focused on answering his questions, eased by the universal curiosity of children. Food began to be carried out from the kitchen: thin slices of meat, hunks of bright cheeses, thick pieces of rye bread, bits of onion doused in vinegar and dill. Every so often Luba and Anna paused their preparations and caressed my shoulders. Liquor bottles appeared, along with shot glasses that clinked as they were set on the table, and I was urged to have "just a little" drink of *horilka.*

When Andriy entered the room, I recognized him immediately from the photographs in the kitchen drawer. He wore a faded blue button-down shirt and dark blue pants. He walked over to Ivan, who was standing near the room's rounded archway, and stretched out his hand. They conversed so quickly and in such muffled tones that I couldn't follow. I watched Andriy glance my way and then urgently speak again to Ivan. He had tears in his eyes.

Andriy moved across the room and kissed Stefa, who was also on the verge of crying. Then he made his way to me. He kissed me firmly on the cheek. "Are you Nadia's daughter or Olga's daughter?" he asked. His voice, baritone and gravelly, had the loud, off-key pitch of an old man with bad hearing. On his forearms, I noticed blurry blue-ink tattoos.

"Nadia's," I said.

"Where is she?" he asked. Where is she?

"She's in Cleveland," I answered. He looked at me uncomprehendingly. "In America," I added, trying to be helpful. Maybe he had never heard of Cleveland.

"In America?" He still looked confused. He turned and looked behind him, and then back at me. "In America? Why isn't she here?"

Oh. "She isn't here," I repeated dumbly. "She couldn't come," I said in a rush. "She couldn't leave America. Too busy." I was a terrible liar.

"Oh." He looked down. "But you are here."

"Yes." The awkwardness I felt was painful. I pulled out a family portrait that I had brought from Stefa's apartment. The photo had been taken a few years earlier for our church directory and in it my family and Olga's family formed a garland of smiling faces around my grandmother and Mr. Sorochak. My grandmother treasured the photograph and my mother had gotten a thick pastel frame for the print they sent to Stefa.

I held the picture steady in front of Andriy. "This is Nadia and this is Olga." I pointed to my mother and my aunt. "They live in Ohio. That is a state." My Ukrainian was still only good enough for elementary conversations, but simple language seemed to suit the moment.

He stared at the photograph. "I can't believe it." Everyone in the room was silent. Each person watched my movements carefully. "This is Nadia?" he asked incredulously, pointing to my mother. "And this is Olga?" He pointed to my aunt.

"Yes, this is Nadia and this is Olga." He didn't look up from the picture. "And this is Al and this is Ron. Al is Nadia's husband

and my father. This is Ron. He is my uncle. This is Alex and Michael. They are my brothers. This is Emerson and Miles. They are my cousins." I moved slowly from face to face, holding my finger on each person as I identified them.

"I can't believe it."

"Alex likes basketball. He just learned to drive." I moved my fists back and forth to mimic driving a car. "Michael likes basketball too. He is a good student; he likes to read a lot." I told Andriy everyone's ages. I didn't have the vocabulary to express that Alex had a routine at dinner in which he would mimic my mother's words and make her laugh but that he had a face as grim as a tombstone in the mornings. Or that Emerson grew his hair out so that it was thick and curly and poofy like my grandmother's probably was when she was younger, because my mother's was like that now. Even if I could have expressed these things in Ukrainian, even if I could have talked forever, I could not have told him everything he needed to know these people.

"I can't believe it."

"My mother is a physical therapist and Olga is a business woman."

"This is Nadia and this is Olga?" He traced the path of my finger as he pointed again at his daughters.

"Yes."

"I can't believe it."

As was typical in Ukraine, a meal had been assembled with no notice. Everyone switched chairs so that I could sit at the head of the table and next to Andriy. Stefa started to tell the group how I wouldn't eat anything at her house. The faces around the table grew solemn. "You must eat now, you are in the house of your grandfather!" urged Anna. I nodded, privately wincing, and grabbed a square caramel cookie off an overflowing bowl and popped it into my mouth. Not that bad.

After about an hour of stilted conversation, Stefa cocked her head at me, indicating that it was time to say goodbye. I wrote the names and ages of all the people in the photograph, so that Andriy could learn them. Luba carefully wrote her name and address in my journal and made me promise to write and send more photographs of my family. After insisting that I wouldn't take money, I accepted a small wooden box as a parting gift, and inside Andriy stuffed a wad of bills he'd been trying to get me to take.

Outside, everyone congregated for a photo. We stood in rows on the porch. When Volodya snapped the picture, I was the only one smiling. Back then, Ukrainians still abided by the Soviet practice of meeting the camera with straight faces.

I hugged Luba and her son and husband. I said that it was nice to meet them. My words felt banal, but I could come up with nothing better. Andriy accompanied us to the car. Near the door, we stopped. "I just wanted you to know that your children have good lives in America," I said to him. "They are happy, they are healthy, they love each other. Everyone is happy." My voice cracked with the last sentence, and I could feel tears forming in the corners of my eyes. It was and was not thanks to him that what I said was true. If he hadn't been so awful, my mother may never have left the Soviet Union. In a way, his awfulness made me.

Andriy shakily kissed me: my cheeks, my arms, my shoulders. He was crying.

"Goodbye," I said. "Thank you."

I waved to the group on the porch and climbed into the car with my family. We made our way back to Stefa's place in a tired silence.

The first thing Stefa did after we had dinner that night was pull out her photo albums. The woman had hundreds of photographs: Volodya as a baby, wrapped up in blankets and being held proudly by my grandmother months before she left for the United States; pictures of Ivan with his children; stills of my mother's childhood. In one, my mother was about six years old, and standing amid the wild grass of Siberia with the man who would become Stefa's husband. The photo's high contrast flattened her cheeks and shrouded her large eyes in darkness. I felt a jolt of recognition. I had never seen a photograph in which she looked so much like me.

Stefa flopped a picture of Andriy in my lap to catch my attention. "Bandriwsky," she said, pronouncing my grandfather's surname sharply. "In Siberia." The photograph was an impromptu
close-up. Andriy was outdoors, perhaps on the deck of the barracks, and wore a traditional Ukrainian blouse. The strong sunlight
defined his features with a precision that made me feel like I was
standing next to him.

She passed me another picture of Andriy, this one of him and
his sister wrapped in warm winter garb. I recognized her immediately from her piercing blue eyes. They stood protectively next to
each other, each one gazing steadily into the camera. "Band-
riwksy." She spit out the name. "In Siberia again." Her tone suggested that she had more to say.

"What do you remember about him?" I asked.

"He was a bad man," she said gravely. "A very, very bad
man."

"But you wanted me to meet him," I said. "Why was he a bad
man?"

The question hung in the air for a moment.

"He did a lot of bad things. Too much *horilka*."

I asked what he did. Stefa hesitated, then continued. "He was
very bad to your grandmother. One time your mother was sick, and
she needed water. Andriy wouldn't let your grandmother go to her.
He told her he would beat her if she did. She had to run a mile in
the snow without shoes to escape from him. She ran to Ivan's. He
hit her often." Stefa clenched her fist and knocked it lightly against
her face.

"He was very bad," she said again, seeing my disturbed response. "Before today, I had not seen him for thirty years. He left
Siberia before I could." She paused. "Another time he had a gun."

"A gun?" I asked, not certain that I understood the word in
Ukrainian.

"Yes, gun," Stefa responded and mock shot at the air in front
of her. "He had a gun and would shoot things off the porch of the
house. But he used it to threaten us. One time he got drunk and shot
through the doors in the house."

"The doors in the house?"

"There were multiple doors, to keep out the cold. And he took the gun and put holes in them, so that the cold could get inside."

I looked down again at the photograph of Andriy resting in my lap. My warm emotions from earlier in the day drained away. I thought: villain, villain, villain.

A week after I returned to the United States, the notorious blackout of 2003 occurred. The day it rolled through Cleveland, I was with my mother in a travel agency where she was questioning a salesman about vacation deals for my parents' twenty-fifth wedding anniversary. While he was talking, the computers shut down, the phones went dead, and the fluorescent lights illuminating the office stopped shining from the ceiling. Embarrassed, the salesman got up from his desk and walked outside. "Did you guys forget to pay your electricity bill?" we heard him ask the counter attendant at the Subway next door.

That evening, as we sat in my parents' dimmed living room, we learned that people from Michigan to Massachusetts had lost power. My dad had turned on a battery-powered radio in the next room, which broadcast accounts of people swarming convenience stores to stock up on bottled water, ice, emergency generators, and canned food. In Ukraine, I had remarked to my family about the darkness of apartment hallways and the streets at night. I could imagine Volodya goading me, "Well, there isn't any light in the U.S. now either!"

As the sun set, the light faded and our surroundings began to disappear into the darkness. At loose ends, my mother and I toured through every possible topic of conversation: movies playing at the mall, my brothers' performance on the basketball team, news about members of my high school class, possibilities for my life after college. When I could no longer see the features on her face, she asked me quietly, "So, Meg, what did my father say?"

The day after I met Andriy, I had called her and recounted the outing. But the night of the blackout, I told her again: He asked for her first. He was touched that I came; he cried when I left. He drank lemon-lime soda. He refused a shot of *horilka*.

"I have such bad memories from my childhood, of him and Mother arguing," she said when I finished. "One time they were fighting and Mother threatened to throw a pan of boiling water on him if he didn't get away from her."

"Did she?" I asked with astonishment.

"I don't remember it very well," she said thoughtfully. "I was pretty little. I must have been in the room when it happened. All I can remember are their faces, how angry they were, and the boiling water on the stove. I think he moved out after that."

"When was the last time you saw him?" I asked.

"After he and Mother got divorced, he would come see me sometimes. I was the youngest, you know." Her tone verged on bashful. "At school, when we went outside to play, sometimes he would be there, on the other side of the fence. He would gesture for me to come over, and pass me some candy through the wire." A flood of sadness washed over me. "I never told anyone," my mother continued. "I never told Mother. I always felt like I was betraying her when I was with him. I was kind of in the middle, you know."

I did know. It was hard to reconcile Andriy's abuse with the kindly, frail old man I had met. I worried that meeting him symbolized on some level that I condoned his behavior, and I came to feel that I had committed an act of betrayal against my grandmother.

I felt that I owed it to her to tell her I had seen Andriy myself, though I was sure Stefa had already conveyed the news. Once power was restored, I drove over to her house in Parma to share photos from my trip.

She was delighted that I could describe to her in competent Ukrainian what each of the pictures showed. As we reached the photos of my visit to Staryava, I mentioned that I had seen Andriy. She rolled her eyes. "*Nu?*" she said. *So what?*

I didn't say anything in response. I saw no reason to risk her anger. If she didn't want to talk about him, that was fine with me.

Apart from a handful of occasions, my grandmother held her silence about my grandfather for the rest of her life. On the rare occasion when she did bring him up, it would be without warning and apropos of nothing. We would be talking about something benign — if her car needed an oil change, for example — when suddenly she would become irritated and say accusingly, "And then you went and saw him."

"Who?" I would ask, although I knew.

"Him — Andriy." And she would say no more. But she didn't need to — I registered her pain, and I carried the guilt of that for years.

We like to believe that experience leads to insight. If I do A, then I will understand A. Sometimes, it works like that. Often, it does not. Sometimes you do A, and then fifteen years later, you understand A, but only because you have also done B, and C, and D, and so on. Or because X or Y or Z has happened. Sometimes you do A and think you understand A, only to realize 15 years later that you were mistaken.

And so it was, fifteen years after I met my grandfather, that I realized at an unrelated, ordinary moment — I was staring at a white brick wall in my local library — that the reason I had wanted to meet him was not to know my grandfather, but to meet my grandmother's former husband, my mother's father. I had wanted to meet him to know them, really.

Like the results of much of my searching, I would understand this too late to plumb the depths of it with my grandmother.

8
A Place Unknown

Life can pivot in a random second. One minute you're travelling from A to B, and the next, you're hiking in the Himalayas.

One evening, when I was visiting my family in Cleveland, my mother and I were relaxing in the family room. A Netflix movie was playing on the TV. My mom was painting her nails. I was on my computer, absent-mindedly surfing the Internet. I Googled "coal mines Chelyabinsk" — Chelyabinsk being the oblast in Siberia where my grandmother had been exiled. I zoomed in on Yeman-zhelinsk, the small settlement more than twenty miles from Chelyabinsk where my had grandparents lived and my mother was born. I Googled "Staryava" and its spellings in Polish and German, "Starzawa" and "Stariawa." I went onto Ukrainian Google and searched Staryava in Cyrillic letters. Nothing new. I came back to the American site. My grandmother's brother wafted into my mind. I punched in "Stefan Mazur Ukraine." A Ukrainian soccer player had the name. I clicked a few links. On a whim, I went back to the search field and added "war." I stopped.

"Mom?" I said nervously, staring at my screen.

I had landed on the digital library of Yad Vashem, Israel's Holocaust memorial complex. A black and white photo of a young man in a uniform hung on my screen. The image was grainy but I could make out his chin, his defined lips, his strong jaw, and the point at the edge of his visible ear. The photo details read that Stefan Mazur had been a policeman in Przemysl, Poland, a regional capital about forty miles away from Staryava.

The title on the page read in part, "Stefan Mazur, a war criminal."

I pushed my laptop screen with its picture of the young man away from me so that my mom could see it. "Do you think this looks like Grandma's Stefan?"

"What?" She looked away from the TV and squinted at the image. "Yeah, maybe."

In my research, I had come across a man named Stefan Mazur who had helped instigate a pogrom against Jewish refugees in the Polish town of Kielce after the war. The violence at Kielce, where forty-two Jews were murdered, sent a shockwave through surviving Jews and led to a surge in their emigration from Poland. Was the Stefan in the photo I was looking at now the same man who had orchestrated the pogroms? I looked more carefully, searching the photo for clues. I couldn't tell.

But I felt a chill. A Ukrainian researcher named Zenon Shandrovich had published a directory of western Ukrainians who fought on behalf of the nationalist movement in the Ukrainian Insurgent Army. I revisited Shandrovich's book in light of my discovery. I knew that Stefan had joined this army, commonly referred to in English by its Ukrainian acronym UPA, at some point after he returned from Germany. The book led to no straightforward conclusions. In fact, it contained two entries for Stepan Mazur, as Stefan would have been remembered by the community:

Stepan Mazur, son of Mykhailo and Rozalia (1920-1947). Joined UPA in 1944. Killed in an ambush in Staryava. Corpse taken to Khyriv and buried on the banks of the Stryazh river.

Stepan Mazur, son of Stepan and Rozalia, pseudonym "Mole" (1923-1945). A member of the Organization of Ukrainian Nationalists and an especially active member of Prosvita. In the village of Orly, in Przemysl region, was a commander of the auxiliary police. Joined the Ukrainian National Union in 1942. In 1944, transferred to a raid battalion. Served in the "Osip" company under the commander "Ren." Participant in the Skole action. In 1945, at the order of Ren, transferred to serve as a field agent, and was active around Staryava. Here he was betrayed by Yaroslav Mocharsky, pseudonym "Winter." Buried in the forest near the village of Tarnavka.

Were these two men the same person? Either could conceivably be my grandmother's brother. The first entry seemed more likely, because the name of both parents was correct. But the source of the second entry could easily have mistaken my great-grandfather Stepan Mazur for Mykhailo—and unlike the first entry, the second recorded the year of Stefan's birth correctly.

Also, there was the matter that Orly, mentioned in the second entry, was a small town outside Przemysl, the site of the photo in the Yad Vashem digital library.

I looked again at the transcripts of the interviews I had done with my grandmother. What was it she had said about Stefan's activities after he left Germany? "He came back here [to Ukraine] and started to work here," she had told me. "Then he went to Lviv because [the Ukrainian nationalist leader] Stepan Bandera was there at that time. They were working with the Germans to build an independent Ukraine. However, he came back from Lviv, and those who stayed there were arrested. He thought he would go to Germany and from there to our father in America. But that organization was created, the organization of partisans [UPA]. He said, 'I'm going to stay here with the boys, to do what needs to be done.'"

What she said made sense at the time. Only when rereading the transcript did I realize that she had not provided any specifics about Stefan's "work" before he joined UPA.

While the Ukrainians of eastern Galicia quickly became wary of the
Germans after they invaded in 1941, they continued to prefer the
Nazis over the Soviets. Ukrainians ranged in their response to the
Holocaust—from sheltering Jews to indifferently observing the violence against them to actively supporting it. The gamut of collaboration in Ukraine was similar to that which occurred in other parts
of occupied Europe, though the extent of popular violence against
Jews, especially in the summer of 1941, was matched in few countries.

To get a better sense of that spectrum of experience, I watched
scores of videotaped testimonies of Holocaust survivors from the
area around Staryava at the Holocaust Museum in Washington.
The Nazis had executed the Holocaust with devastating success in
eastern Galicia. Few Jews survived. The testimonies were full of
hellish stories of terror and deprivation in ghettos, camps, forests,
cellars.

This wasn't a surprise, but it still shook me that many survivors felt a pointed anger at Ukrainians, portraying them as the most
brutal of the ethnic groups that had a hand in the Holocaust. "The
Ukrainians were absolute sadists," declared one female survivor.
"They were vicious. They were absolutely terrible," remembered
another. "Whatever they had to do, they did a hundred times
worse." In several cases, the subjects evinced more hatred of
Ukrainians than of the Germans themselves. One survivor who by
the 1990s had settled in California said that if a Ukrainian applied
for a job at his office, he wouldn't hire him. But "the Germans? The
majority—I can tolerate them." Another survivor was even less for-
giving. "I wish Stalin were still alive so he could take all of the
Ukrainians and slaughter them like cattle," the man said. "I don't
care what they have today, democracy or whatever. They killed
most of the Ukrainian Jews."

The experiences reached me in a new way when I came across
the audio recordings of a Chicago psychologist named David P.
Boder. In 1946, a year after Roosevelt, Churchill, and Stalin met at
Yalta to arrange the postwar reorganization of Europe, Boder, a Jew
who had been born in Latvia, made his way to Europe to interview

residents of camps for displaced persons. In doing so, he produced the earliest audio recordings of Holocaust victims, preserving the voices of the victims at a moment when their suffering was still very recent. His work was powerful. As I clicked through his recordings, I realized that after watching so many testimonies videotaped many decades after the fact, I had in some way started to think of the Holocaust as something that happened only to the elderly.

Not surprisingly, the Boder interview that rattled me most was the only one he conducted with a child. Raisel Meltzak, age thirteen, was living in a home for displaced Jewish orphans in 1946 when she crossed paths with Boder and his wire recorder. Though the orphanage had diagnosed Raisel with intellectual disability, she spoke Yiddish rapidly, with eagerness and impulsiveness.

Like all of the testimonies, her story was horrific.

Raisel hailed from Busk, a small town with Polish, Ukrainian, and Jewish residents located about a hundred miles northeast of Staryava. When the Germans invaded, she told Boder, her family hid in a hole in a stable and exchanged their valuables for meager rations, delivered in secret by a local Christian woman. At night, they faced extortion from residents of the town. After two weeks in the pit, the woman informed them that the Germans were inspecting the area with dogs and the family fled. Before the Meltzaks got away, the Ukrainians robbed them of everything but the clothes on their backs. Even their coats, Raisel specified.

Raisel's father left the forest, perhaps for the safety of the ghetto. They did not see him again. The rest of the family took refuge in the forest, staying on the move to avoid capture. But the Ukrainian police discovered Raisel and her mother and beat them with horse whips. Though they survived, the forest proved to be its own menace: Raisel's three-year-old brother succumbed to starvation. Her mother went mad with grief and soon died.

Boder stopped the interview at that point, noting that he believed Raisel was deeply traumatized, not intellectually disabled as the orphanage had stated.

A deadening, concrete dread filled my stomach. As much as I searched, I couldn't figure out what happened to Raisel.

By most accounts, a distant but unaffected tolerance between the ethnic groups prevailed in rural eastern Galician outposts like Staryava before the war. Most people in Staryava were ethnically Ukrainian, but there were sizable Polish and Jewish minorities. Each group viewed the other as different, but they did interact, and through these exchanges forged a functioning community. Ukrainian, Polish, and Jewish children all studied together in the village school, and when the Ukrainian or Polish priest arrived for religious instruction, the students of other ethnicities would calmly pack up their bags and leave the room. It was just how things were done. Writing about a Ukrainian village close to Staryava, the historian Leonid Heretz concluded that Ukrainians saw Jews "as a fundamentally, ontologically different people, but also as people who had always been in the village." They were "part of the traditional fabric of life."

The few Jews from my grandmother's area who survived the war and shared their stories expressed similar feelings about Ukrainians before the Germans took over in 1941. Ben Teicher, who came from a well-off Jewish farming family in the village of Torczynowice, also heavily Ukrainian, said, "No, there was no bitterness.... Before the war, there was no strong anti-Semitism." "The Ukrainians and Jews got along well," Aunt Nastka had told me. "I don't remember anything different." As a girl, my grandmother would get a bit of sugar from the Jews of Staryava in exchange for lighting a match for them to start a fire on the Sabbath. After Passover, the village children went from home to home to collect plain matzos the Jews would give them for free — it was "like Halloween," she said.

Even so, tension lurked beneath the surface, fed by long-ingrained social structures that granted advantages to some groups while withholding them from others. Tensions were also aggravated by that timeless irritant — petty differences. My grandmother remembered feeling ashamed when as a girl she accepted a piece of candy from a Jewish neighbor only to be told after she had eaten it that she had to pay up. There was a circuitous dynamic to the resentments: Ukrainians and Jews resented the Poles' authority over all things governmental; the Poles resented the Ukrainians' defiance; the Ukrainians and Poles resented the Jews' success in business and suspected they exploited their position for personal gain. The stories each group told itself about the others exaggerated these differences, making the tensions even worse. "The Jews would sell you a bottle of vodka, write that you bought three, and then take your fields and drive you out of the house," one elderly Staryava resident told me more than sixty years after the end of the war.

From Staryava's listing in the Polish business directory of 1929, I could see that the Jews in the village were merchants and farmers and people who devoted themselves to religious study and prayer. They worked at the stone quarry and the sawmill. They sold tobacco. I traded emails with a woman in Israel whose grandparents had run a small store in Staryava. She wrote me that her grandfather was a "gentle religious person who studied the bible all day long and was not good in commerce." Her grandmother took charge of the store, and she kept her toddler son "busy at her side in an empty pickle barrel." Though it's hard to believe that the peasants would have indulged in such a luxury, a dentist was even among them—a man named Monek Kirshner offered dental services in the village, according to the testimonials about Holocaust victims submitted to Yad Vashem.

That's what's left of the Jews of Staryava—names and basic details that relatives submitted to Yad Vashem's Central Database of Shoah Victims' Names, an attempt to save the approximately six million Jews killed in the Holocaust from obscurity. Several Jews from Staryava are listed in the registry, including Regina Augarten, an eighteen-year-old woman reportedly killed in Staryava in 1942; her parents, Herman and Tonia; her older brothers, Jacob and Meir; and her older sister, Fani. It also preserved the names of Blima Felsen, a housewife; the Weiss brothers—Romek, Lezer, and Moishe—

teenagers when they were killed; Wolf Zupnik; and Chaska, Cyla, and Shoshanna Olech.

I spent one long afternoon typing all the names I had compiled of Staryava's Jews into the ITS database to see if I could find records suggesting that any of them survived the war or, at the very least, details about their fates. I found virtually nothing.

The absence of documentation, it turns out, makes a certain kind of sense. In autumn 1941, a few months after Germany reneged on the terms of the Molotov-Ribbentrop Pact and invaded the Soviet Union, the Nazis launched a plan to exterminate the Jews of Poland—Operation Reinhard. It called for the majority to be massacred at new camps designed exclusively for killing. Because the intent of these camps was so clearly exterminatory, the Nazis dispensed with the practice of registering their victims. When they arrived, the Jews were sent summarily to the gas chambers. No one bothered to take their names.

Other details suggest, however, that the Jews of Staryava were murdered much closer to home. The Soviet Union's patchwork rail system made transporting large numbers of people difficult. Accordingly, the Nazis created mobile killing units that systematically roamed the steppe, forcing Jews from their homes, marching them to the outskirts of their village or town, and executing them in a hail of gunfire. Their bodies fell into pits that some of the victims themselves had been forced to dig; men might be kept alive to bury the bodies and then they, too, would be shot. Patrick Debois, a French priest who spearheads an effort to document and memorialize this wave of murders, estimates that more than 1.5 million Jews died in this "Holocaust by bullets."

The mystery of the fate of the Jews of Staryava was solved when I met an elderly Staryava resident named Stefania Midyanka. Born in 1928 to an ethnic Ukrainian family, Stefania was thirteen when the Nazis took over. I visited her one afternoon in the company of some young World War II researchers from Lviv's Territory of Terror Museum. Their high-tech video camera, which they used to record an interview with Stefania for their archive of oral histories, looked out of place in her living room, whose worn floral-patterned couch seemed to have been in place for decades.

Though Stefania had already marked her ninetieth birthday, she spoke at length and with admirable clarity about the tumultuous history that had shaped her life. And she was playful. When the researchers asked her to sign a release permitting the interview to be stored in their database, she took the pen and joked, "Like in the collective farm?" The Soviets had made a big deal of the paperwork around collective farms, apparently.

Growing up, Stefania told us, she had lived on a property that shared a fence with the local Jewish prayer house. Stefania remembered it as a solemn space, with separate prayer rooms for men and women and a place for people to wash their feet. She listed the surnames of the Jewish families and businesses they had operated in the village. The names hung in the air of her living room for a moment after she said them.

The butchers Homka and Orhatyn.

Zinger and Friedman, who sold *horilka*.

Hausen and Zhupnik, who operated grocery stores.

Gottlieb, who owned the quarry.

Vilyus, the barber.

At school, Stefania said, she was friendly with a Jewish girl named Frida who was about her age and lived nearby.

When the Nazis took over, they turned the prayer house into a ghetto, imprisoning Jews from Staryava and other neighboring villages. Guards policed the property. The Staryava Jews had been imprisoned for about three months when, one evening, Stefania's family's dog started barking uncontrollably. Stefania's father went outside to calm him and found the garden swarming with Nazis. One of them told him to take the dog inside and shut him up. That night, a ghastly wailing came from the ghetto. The family dared not leave the house to investigate.

The next morning was eerily calm. The deed was done: The Jews had been forced to a pit outside the village and shot; then, their bodies were covered with lime. Stefania was part of a group of children who made their way to the site a few days later to gawk

at the upturned earth. "Frida is lying there," she said unemotion-
ally.

Eventually, Stefania's family moved into the house Frida and
her family had been forced from. They remain there today. Bewildering details like this are shared matter-of-factly by Staryava residents; the realities of survival are no surprise to anyone. Families
moved into the houses of those who had been shot, deported, or
sent to a concentration camp without much of a second thought.
Even my family's property in Staryava was subject to this treatment. After the Mazurs were exiled to Siberia, Rozalia and Mike's
house, the one they had worked so hard to finance and build, was
lifted off its foundation and deposited on a plot of land a few miles
away where another family installed themselves.

After we wound up our interview that day, the researchers
and I took a short walk with Stefania through her garden to the old
prayer house, which had been abandoned long ago. Stefania's
great-grandchildren trailed behind us, shyly observing their visitors from a distance. The gray building bore the typical signs of neglect—on the facade, parts of the mortar had cracked and fallen
away, revealing the uneven bricks beneath. Weeds grew up the
walls.

At one point after the war, the prayer house was a sausage
shop, Stefania told us; then, it was a cafeteria for Soviet workers. A
faded sign bearing a Soviet emblem and the Ukrainian word for
canteen still hung near a heavy wooden door. The structure had always had problems, though—mold, bad floors. "It was a house of
prayer, not a house of life," Stefania said. A man doing repairs on
the building quit after he claimed he saw a woman in white walking on the roof one night. Stefania had teased him about it, but he
refused to see it as a laughing matter. His seriousness chastened
her. "It's clear that there is this kind of thing in the world," she said
with a knowingness that seemed possible only from the vantage
point of her many years.

The Nazis, of course, had not carried out massacres in villages like
Staryava on their own. Many Ukrainians were enthusiastic about

the Nazi regime, especially initially, and the Germans sought ways to make formal use of it. They had an obvious need: The conquest of Soviet territory gave the Germans a broad swath of new land to administer. A sizable police force was needed to guard government buildings and military installations, enforce curfews, and crack down on a black market that was thriving in the midst of wartime scarcity and government requisitions. The service of locals made keeping these areas in check a lot easier.

Of course, the Germans didn't need help only with typical municipal functions. They needed help with the Final Solution. What became known as the Ukrainian auxiliary police were integral to Hitler's plan to exterminate the Jews. Two scholars of the region writing jointly called this force "the institutional epicenter of Ukrainian collusion with the Nazis." The police force became the foot soldiers of the Holocaust in eastern Galicia—they registered Jews; policed Jews in the ghettos; searched homes, ghettos, and forests for Jews in hiding; and imprisoned Jews prior to their deportation and execution. In numerous cases, they directly participated in massacres. "The Ukrainian police was bathing itself in Jewish blood. They searched through every godforsaken hole. They crawled into every nook where only a human being could possibly hide, using pocket flashlights to light it up," remembered one survivor of the liquidation of the Jewish ghetto in Lviv.

Ukrainian auxiliary police were present in Staryava. Stefania remembered seeing the yellow-and-blue armbands they wore over their uniforms. The night the Jews were forced from the ghetto, the man who had yelled at Stefania's father about their barking dog— that man had spoken in Ukrainian. The typical Nazi did not know Ukrainian. The detail suggested that locals (likely the auxiliary police) helped round up the Jews (and possibly helped kill them.)

I increasingly suspected that my grandmother's beloved brother Stefan had been among their ranks.

Several pieces lined up. There was the entry in the Shandrovich book that had a Stefan Mazur serving as an auxiliary policeman outside Przemysl. There was the photo of "war criminal" Stefan Mazur, the Ukrainian policeman photographed in Przemysl.

And the date of our Stefan Mazur's return to Ukraine coincided with the Nazis' efforts to recruit young Ukrainian men into the Ukrainian police. According to the documents from Stefan's stay in Germany, the last time the Nazi bureaucracy observed him in Braunschweig was June 7, 1941, a few weeks before the surprise German invasion of the Soviet Union. By April 15, 1942, Stefan was officially noted to have departed for "a place unknown." If he had joined the police by the spring of 1942, Stefan, then aged nineteen, would have been poised to help Operation Reinhard reach its grisly climax in his native region.

By June 1943, thanks in no small part to the Ukrainian police, the vast majority of Jews in eastern Galicia were dead.

I was having difficulty wrapping my head around my own suspicions, so I sought to speak to all the relatives I could about Stefan. I reached out to Slavik, my grandmother's first cousin, to see if I could interview him, as he had known Stefan as a child. Slavik was a Mazur from Staryava—the son of one of Mykhailo's brothers—and because his father had been active in UPA, Slavik's immediate family had also been exiled to Siberia. At the time of their exile, Slavik had been in fourth grade.

My mom and I were visiting Stefa at her apartment in Truskavets when Slavik and I spoke. Inspired by my travels, my mom had started occasionally joining me on trips to Ukraine. While certain things jarred her—the periodic water shortages, the unkempt landscaping, the shots of *horilka* at lunch—she stepped into life there easily. The family we visited were, after all, often people she had grown up with, and the bonds showed.

Slavik lived close by, just seven minutes on foot from Stefa through a maze of unlit alleys. He was a short man with silver hair and pink skin. His eyes were Mazur blue, big and bold and the color of robin's eggs. He had a sense of mischievousness about him, as if from his head of silver hair there should curl the telltale cowlick of a boy up to no good.

There was a bit of tension in the air that day. Slavik and Stefa had quarreled recently; Stefa had forgotten Slavik's birthday and he had taken umbrage. "Who does he think he is, Barack Obama?" Stefa had growled, annoyed, when telling me the story.

Slavik sat on the couch in Stefa's living room, his knees together, and looked at me expectantly. Feeling a surge of self-consciousness, I looked down at my notes and asked him about his current circumstances. Slavik reported that he was living off his pension. "Sometimes I go to Staryava and around Lviv Oblast."

"Do you go by car?"

"No, I don't drive anymore." He had been a bus driver in Soviet times. "I don't have a car, and I don't have a bicycle."

"You have a bicycle," Stefa said, plunking a dish of hard-boiled eggs and pickles on the table before us.

"The bicycle is broken," Slavik objected to Stefa's retreating back.

I showed him some of the photos I had. "This is my grandmother. What do you remember?"

"That's my cousin," he agreed, looking at the photograph. He nudged my mom and smiled. "You are the same as when you were a child," he said. He had known her as a schoolgirl in Siberia. I knew what he meant; my mom had a natural good-naturedness. I could see traces of it in photographs of her when she was a kid—the camera always seemed to capture her wearing a kindly look, her eyebrows softly raised.

My mom laughed. "How many kids do you have?" she asked.

"I have a son and a daughter but I don't have any grandchildren. My son doesn't want to get married. My daughter lives in Kyiv. She is married but she and her husband don't have their own place, and that's why she doesn't want a baby. That's my situation. I want grandchildren." Turning to me, he said, "Maybe you can stay here as my granddaughter. Will you stay?"

I kept quiet—I had not prepared for this question in my notes.

"She isn't listening to me," he said to my mom.

"She is serious. She has questions to ask," my mom said.

I cleared my throat. "What are your earliest memories?"

"I remember the war. I remember the sound of shooting and people being killed as I was bringing food to the rebels. It was war, as wars are."

"What was it like when the Germans came?"

"It was horrible how many people were killed here. Simple people, simple Germans, didn't take anything from us. But there was also the Gestapo, like the Russian KGB. Simple soldiers walked around the village to buy or exchange things for eggs or sour cream. They cracked the eggs into a bucket, added lots of sour cream and honey or sugar, and mixed it all together. They called it 'Gogol Mogol.' If there were kids there, they gave the kids the first taste. That's 100 percent the truth. But there were fascists, too. God."

"You know, we don't know a lot about Stefan," my mom said. I pulled out a copy of the photo of Stefan.

"He was in Germany first and then in UPA," I offered. "Do you know what he was up to?"

Slavik peered at the photo. "Yes, I remember. He was a captain, a military judge. UPA had security services, like the KGB. They had special troops for things like presidential security, spying. He was in the counterespionage services, and he was a judge. He judged people who did bad things. He even had to sentence a friend to death."

"What happened?" I asked.

"People received parcels from America. Some of the parcels had a special kind of scarf in them. This guy, Slavko, went to a person's house and stole one of the scarves. Slavko and Stefan had gone to school together. He was even distantly related to us. He was a nice guy. But he was judged and shot. Stefan gave him the death penalty."

"They shot him because he stole a scarf?"

"Yes, yes, it was forbidden. He had committed a robbery. At the time, they were really strict."

I wasn't sure what to do with this information. "Was Stefan a good person?" I finally asked. It was a silly question, an impossible question, yet it was what I wanted to know.

"Stefan? Yes, he was good. He was observing the law. If he hadn't done that, they would have killed him. Slavko was guilty. He went to that house and sinned. Stefan is not guilty, it was Slavko who was guilty."

I was struggling mightily; nothing seemed to make sense. Why would Stefan serve the Nazis after returning from working in the Reich, where conditions for foreign workers were so notoriously bleak that men absconded all the time? If Stefan's time in Braunschweig had been miserable enough, it seemed to me that he would have wanted to have nothing to do with the Germans. I wrote a historian who had written a seminal study on foreign labor in the Reich to see what he thought.

The professor responded quickly. "Your uncle came to Germany very early as a volunteer, which suggests a very pro-German or even pro-Nazi stance," he wrote. "That he would then join the [German cause] corresponds to a frequent pattern."

"Interesting career," he added. "But probably a pretty terrible story."

Probably a pretty terrible story. With these words, a darkness fell over Stefan that would never quite lift in my mind. For so long he had been a figure of beneficence, of mercy. But now a different picture was emerging.

9

In the Archives

Having exhausted my extended family's tranche of memories, I decided to dig deeper into the archives. I yearned for the authority of the written word. Documents had their flaws, but at least they were frozen in time and shielded from the vagaries of fading memory.

I arranged to spend a few days in Lviv, where documents about my family were liable to be held. It was a good time to try to obtain them. After maintaining a close hold on sensitive personal documents for years after the fall of the Soviet Union, the Ukrainian government had steadily liberalized access to its archives. The shift reflected the country's changing political allegiances. In early 2014, after the sitting Ukrainian president, Viktor Yanukovych, fled to Russia following his government's bloody suppression of mass demonstrations in favor of European integration and against police brutality, a new, more European-minded president, Petro Poroshenko, had been elected, and his tenure ushered in all sorts of changes.

Yanukovych's bloody crackdown and Russia's subsequent invasion of eastern Ukraine and Crimea enflamed Ukrainian nationalism and anti-Soviet sentiment. Under Poroshenko's leadership, the government implemented a package of "decommunization" laws to officially burn the Soviet hold on Ukrainian historical memory. Among them was the most expansive public access to archives of a past totalitarian regime on the books in Europe.

The government poured resources into making case files created about Ukrainian citizens accessible. For those yearning to see such files (a small cohort, admittedly), the changes were a boon. All I had to do was send a person's name and a few vital statistics to the archive email address and, within two months, I would be clicking through a carefully scanned copy of the file the KGB or another Soviet police organ had kept on that person. After the fall of the Soviet Union, the KGB rebranded itself as the Security Service of Ukraine, the Sluzhba Bezpeky Ukrayiny (SBU). I sent so many of these requests to the director of the SBU archives that he friended me on Facebook.

My feelings about these developments were mixed. On one hand, it was incredibly moving to see the stories of those who had suffered for decades in state-mandated silence. On the other, it seemed that the government wanted to advertise Ukrainians' victimhood at the hands of the Soviets as widely as possible for political reasons all its own. While the openness impressed me, it also seemed somewhat reckless. It didn't matter whether I was related to the subject of the file. It didn't matter if the individuals I was asking about were still living. It didn't matter what I wanted to do with the information. The policy raised all sorts of concerns about privacy, but I was a pragmatist at the end of the day and wanted to work with what I could get. Needless to say, I was also very curious.

Some records remained out of reach, perhaps because they suggested a more complicated take on Ukrainian nationalism. Anecdotes from researchers indicated that the personnel files on the Ukrainian police under the Nazis, for example, were still hard, if not impossible, to access. Other records got caught up in classification procedures that had precedence over the decommunization law. In short, even with unprecedented access, there were still plenty of documents beyond the reach of a simple email.

My flurry of emails netted some interesting finds, including case files on two of my great-grandfather Mykhailo's brothers who had been captured in Staryava while fighting for UPA. But they hadn't yielded anything on Mykhailo's son Stefan or the time my grandmother, mother, and other family members spent in exile in Siberia, another aspect of my family's past that I wanted to investigate. I decided it was time for a visit to Lviv.

While I was in the city, I stayed with Lida, a cousin of some remove who was about my age. It was Lida, her younger sister, Ira, and another girl cousin of ours who appeared in the family photos I used to study at my grandmother's house, all of them wearing clothes of mine that I had outgrown. In my suitcase, I had two ten-packs of Big Red chewing gum to give her. My grandmother used to include the gum in the packages she sent to Ukraine in the 1980s and 90s. Lida had mentioned once how much she enjoyed the gum and how much she missed it — it was one of the few Western candy brands still unavailable in Ukraine. To her, Big Red had "the taste of childhood," she said.

When I had visited Ukraine for the first time in 2003, Lida was still in high school. She was quiet and wore her dark blonde hair in a bob with long bangs that slid over one eye. Now Lida was in her late twenties, and her life was surprisingly familiar to me. She shared an apartment with two roommates. She had a nose ring, and a job she wasn't crazy about — as a customer service rep for a mobile phone company — but it was okay for now. She stayed up late looking at things on the Internet. She met her friends in the city center for happy hour. When asked about men, she would sigh and duck the question. Tacked on her bedroom wall was a list of cities around the world she wanted to visit. A few of them — Budapest, Prague, Vienna — had checks next to them.

Lida lived south of the city center, in a typical five-story Soviet-era apartment building. The neighborhood was filled with worn buildings like hers, but still it pulsed with life, community, intent. Thick trees lined the streets. Ukrainians of all ages hurried along the sidewalks — young men with buzzcuts and black leather jackets striding authoritatively, their hands sunk into their pockets; women with highlights a shade or three too blond; old ladies with their heads covered with babushkas, hauling large plastic bags fashioned in plaid; children strolling indolently behind their parents, the girls with their long hair in braids.

The first morning of my visit, Lida stood in her kitchen, looking at me uncertainly. What did I want for breakfast? Cold cuts? Cereal? Tomatoes? Muesli? Kasha? Yogurt? Pizza? She could make anything.

"Muesli and yogurt would be great," I told her. She looked at me unhappily. That was definitely not enough. Surely I needed bread, at least.

Ukrainian bureaucracy was formidable, especially for a foreigner, so I hired a local archival specialist to help me grease the wheels. I had arranged to meet the archivist that morning at the building housing the SBU's regional archives. Lida accompanied me there, and we met the archivist, a cheery middle-aged man with a tidy European-manufactured SUV, on a sidewalk near the SBU headquarters. Inside, we had a quick meeting with a stern bureaucrat who dispatched any notion that the archive might have any materials about Stefan. (Later, of course, I would discover that the official was wrong.)

Discouraged, I directed us on toward our next target: documents related to my family's exile to Siberia in 1947. I knew by then that it had occurred under the auspices of Operation West, an effort by the Soviets to undermine support for the Ukrainian nationalist movement by deporting its prime constituency — family members of UPA fighters — from western Ukraine, the movement's stronghold. Ukrainians deported under Operation West were sent to various undesirable pockets of the Soviet Union, from Karaganda Oblast, in Kazakhstan; to Volodga Oblast, in western Russia; to Chita Oblast, in Siberia's bleak heart. My family ended up in a nascent coal-mining settlement called Yemanzhelinsk, just east of the Ural Mountains in western Siberia.

The Soviets euphemistically called the communities where they banished the deportees "special settlements," but they were only special in a negative sense. In keeping with the broader gulag system of which they were part, the special settlements were designed to separate and punish those who resisted the Soviet regime.

Once we left the SBU headquarters, the archivist drove Lida and me to Lviv's historic center, where the state archives were kept in a seventeenth century arsenal that had been constructed to store armaments in the event of a Turkish invasion. We walked through a pretty courtyard into the reception area. Lida and I sat in a dark and drafty hallway while the archivist spoke with one of his contacts. After a time, the door opened at the end of the hallway and light beamed onto us.

"No files here," said a young uniformed man. "We only have files on Operation Vistula." Operation Vistula was a different post-war mass deportation, in which more than a million Poles and Ukrainians were resettled within the boundaries of their corresponding nation states. "The Ministry of Internal Affairs probably has them," the young man added. So we piled into the archivist's SUV and drove a mile through the bumpy cobblestone streets of the center and up a hill where the regional archives of the Ministry of Internal Affairs were located.

The archivist quickly made inroads with the personnel at the archive. "Are you sure you want to stay?" I asked Lida before I followed him into the office where we planned to explain our request. Visiting the KGB headquarters, then the state archives, and now the Internal Affairs archives had taken hours, and I knew she was taking time off from work to chaperone me. I felt guilty, but I also knew that I was thinking like an American. The pace of Ukrainian life was slower and less addled than what I was used to; if a friend stopped by for tea, the visit could last three hours, not forty-five minutes. And the American penchant for individualism had little traction in Ukraine. In the United States, people gave great leeway to individuals' preferences and interests, but you were left to navigate a lot on your own. In Ukrainian culture, virtually nothing trumped helping family — even if you insisted that the help was not needed.

Lida just nodded at me, sat down in a wooden chair outside the office, and pulled out her Kindle.

The archivist launched into an account of why we were there — that we wanted to view the files on the Mazur family of Staryava, who had been subject to deportation as part of Operation West. The archivist kept his hands folded on the table as he spoke. His tone carried a hint of the obsequious. He was good. The official looked at us skeptically, but wrote down the names of my family members, then walked out of the room.

The archivist and I sat alone in the bright room and waited. Bare tree branches gently tapped against the window, which looked out onto a cobblestone street. The archivist explained in a

low voice that the ministry was notoriously guarded about its holdings and might not grant me access to the files even if it had them.
After a while, in the corridor where Lida was sitting, I saw a woman
with a ream of yellowed documents walking in the direction where
the official had gone.

The official returned. "We do have documents relating to the
individuals you named: Rozalia Mazur, Ivan Mazur, Anna Bandriwska, Andriy Bandriwsky, and Stefa Punko." I smiled. "But you
need to complete an application to receive access to the documents,
as well as provide documentation showing your relationship to the
subjects in the files."

"I have my grandmother's birth certificate," I said, as if that
could satisfy her terms. However, despite the fact that I had made
this trip to Ukraine explicitly to visit archives, I hadn't brought it
with me. In the bustle of packing, I had forgotten it in Washington,
where it was in a Ziploc bag in my desk drawer. The birth certificate
was a piece of my grandmother's history and I guarded it carefully.
While it wasn't the original, I nonetheless treasured it because it
was from my grandmother's time in the Soviet Union and showed
her place of birth in pretty Cyrillic script. We had so few items that
physically testified to her life before she came to America.

"Well, all that says is that she was born," the official retorted.
She explained that to access the files I needed to establish that I was
my grandmother's direct descendant—an exercise that would require my mother's birth certificate, evidence of her marriage to my
father, and my own birth certificate, all translated into Ukrainian
and notarized. Compiling all that would take forever, and then I'd
have to somehow transmit it to the ministry when I was back in the
U.S. I scowled at the official.

"Is there a way that I can help?" Lida asked. She had risen
from the chair and moved into the doorway. "Could I write the application and provide the documentation?" The official shrugged.
As the granddaughter of Ivan, my grandmother's younger brother,
Lida was no further removed from the people in the files than I was.
Her family's documents were in Ukrainian, moreover, and she
could easily get what we needed from her mother, who lived in a

coal-mining town about forty-five miles outside of Lviv. The official gave us instructions for how to file the application; we would, of course, have to do it in a different building on the other side of the city.

Lida, the archivist, and I walked out of the building onto the sidewalk. The archivist lit a clove cigarette. "I will tell you an old joke," he said. "We used to call the Lyubyanka the tallest building in the Soviet Union. Why?" He studied our blank faces for a moment. The Lyubyanka was the notorious Moscow headquarters of the KGB, and the site of countless coercive interrogations, executions, and acts of torture. "Because even from its basement, you could see Siberia."

Lida's mother offered to get the documents to us that day. I took that to mean that she was going to come to Lviv herself that afternoon to deliver them, and I winced at the thought of yet another relative of mine making a long trip solely on my behalf, and with so little notice, though such an act would have been in keeping with my family's unrelenting support. The cheapest and most common mode of transportation for such a trip would be a public van or minibus called *marshrutka* that followed established routes. The accommodations were hardly luxurious but what made the trip a real hardship was the poor quality of the roads. Even well-traveled thoroughfares were riddled with potholes, and drivers had to weave slowly down the street to avoid them. What should be an hour trip could balloon to three hours if conditions were at their worst.

Lida explained, to my relief, that her mother wasn't going to make the trip herself; she would pay a driver of a *marshrutka* heading to Lviv a small fee to transport the documents—it was a Ukrainian version of a same-day messenger service. We would have what we needed that afternoon.

Lida required her own passport to complete the application, so the archivist drove us back to her apartment to pick it up. By late afternoon, we were in a large, smelly parking lot in the southern part of the city that served as the staging ground for the vans that ventured outside Lviv. The archivist stayed in his car while Lida and I trudged through the narrow lanes between the vehicles, checking the dirt-flecked windows for a placard bearing the number Lida's mother had given her.

"Oh, there it is," Lida said as she watched a *marshrutka* turn and barrel toward the opposite end of the parking lot. She ran in the direction of the dirty minivan, me in her wake. She doubled back to me with the documents before I even reached the van. "We're all set," she said and grinned, brandishing a Ziploc bag of documents.

We submitted the request for the files in the waning minutes of the workday. The ministry where we had to file the request was in a stately building not far from the university where I studied Ukrainian on my first trip to the country. Lida got a sheet of paper from one of the staff and in careful Cyrillic script wrote a statement requesting the files, each line of text equally spaced after the other, a relic of her time in the school system of newly independent Ukraine, where the Soviet belief in good penmanship had still been an article of faith.

The official accepted Lida's written statement and took photocopies of the documents. We would hear back in seven to ten days, she said. By that time, I would be back in the United States, but Lida assured me that of course it would be no problem for her to retrieve whatever the archive found.

Successfully filing the request felt like a victory, so I took some time to just hang out. Lida's younger sister, Ira, also lived in Lviv, where she worked in tourism and did art on the side. The three of us walked around Lviv's picturesque center, weaving in and out of its shops, boutiques, and restaurants, keeping our eyes peeled for "ghost signs" — remnants of advertisements in Polish or Yiddish that hinted at the time when Ukrainians were a minority in the city — and buildings whose doors were ajar so that we could step into their foyers and gawk at their elegant floor tiles, banisters, and light fixtures. There was no need to plan for these stops; in Lviv, small, everyday beauty was everywhere.

I was constantly marveling at all the ways Ukraine had changed since I began visiting in 2003, more than a decade earlier. The Barbie aesthetic cultivated by many Ukrainian women — high heels, short skirts, sequins — had been supplanted by a hipster look of sneakers, piercings, and tattoos. Ukrainian men had added color to their wardrobes, grown out their hair, and discarded pointy-toed dress shoes and stiff black leather jackets. Ryanair and other low-cost airlines now flew out of a handful of Ukrainian cities to European destinations, benefiting Ukrainians who, after years of enduring lengthy and costly paperwork, had been able since 2017 to travel to the Schengen Area, a visa-free zone comprising twenty-six European countries. Perhaps most importantly, every quarter of public life was now inhabited by young people who either had no memory of the Soviet era or had been born after it ended.

While we waited for drinks at a bar that night, Lida taught me Ukrainian neologisms for American business terms — *kanseliuvaty* meant to cancel, *skipnuty* meant to skip. The next day, when she struggled with the web version of her Microsoft Outlook mailbox, I took a look at it and pointed her to the tile she needed to click. With that, her calendar unfurled before her, a familiar cascade of blue rectangles. They were marked with English terms that could have been drawn from my own office life: "performance evaluation," "catch up," "training session."

My last night in town, we stayed up late sharing our favorite YouTube videos: mine, Lady Gaga singing for Mexican orphans; Lida's, a schlubby American guy who sang like an angel; and Ira's, five people using a single guitar to play "Somebody That I Used to Know." I thought of our grandparents, Anna and Ivan, who experienced their homeland as a place of oppression, violence, and deep poverty, and who spent the second half of their lives on different continents, separated by an iron curtain. For them, this positive, everyday point of connection would have been no small achievement.

The next morning, Lida decided to *skipnuty* her first meeting so she could see me off at the airport. Before we left the apartment, she crouched to the floor, a Ukrainian tradition before a big trip, and gestured for me to join her. I obediently sank down. In keeping with the tradition, we said nothing. For a few seconds, we stared at our toes and yielded to the power of ritual, to the changing of time and place and circumstance, to inhabiting with intention the moment between the settled past and the unknown future. I wondered whether my mother and grandmother had observed the practice before they left the Soviet Union more than fifty years earlier. For a fleeting moment, it seemed like they were with us, their hands pulling at their ankles, their chins resting on their folded knees.

"Okay, that's enough," Lida said, breaking the silence. We grabbed the handles of my bags and headed down the stairs. The Uber was waiting.

The Nazis spent three years ruling Staryava before the tides of war turned once again. In 1944, after months of planning, the U.S. and British Commonwealth forces landed on the beaches of Normandy while the Soviets executed a major offensive in Belarus. Nazi resolve weakened, just as the two Allies had hoped. Before launching their plan, the United States, the United Kingdom, and the Soviet Union had reached agreements that ultimately had the effect of dividing Europe into two spheres of influence not long after the Nazi defeat—ironically, largely along a line drawn as part of the 1939 Molotov-Ribbentrop Pact. Galicia ended up being split in half once more, with the eastern part, which included Staryava, again becoming part of the Ukrainian Soviet Socialist Republic. The western part of Galicia become part of Poland. This time, the order would hold not just for a few years but for almost half a century.

The Soviets started to push west in the summer of 1944. The Germans did not go peacefully. In their last days in Staryava, they destroyed the village's few notable pieces of infrastructure, blowing up the bridge over the Stryazh River and setting fire to the timber factory. The ground shook with bombs. When the fighting got particularly fierce, parents sent their children into the woods to sleep.

The return of the villagers' former Soviet overlords brought fresh fears. People who had helped the Germans now had a target on their backs. The man who had served as the head of the village council under the Germans got twenty-five years in a gulag labor camp. So did the man who had replaced him. With prospects like this, many who had been cozy with the Nazi regime scrambled to leave, as did those who had any reason to fear a Soviet takeover. About 120,000 western Ukrainians trailed the retreating Nazi line as refugees. Most of them ended up in displaced persons camps before immigrating to countries all over the world.

The reinstatement of Soviet power was agonizing for many Ukrainians in eastern Galicia for another reason. Many had hoped that a new twist in the war's chaos might provide just the opening for an independent Ukrainian state to form. Different strains of nationalism had circulated in Ukraine before and during the first years of the war. By the time the Soviets retook western Ukraine in 1944, however, the more radical variant of the paramilitary Organization of Ukrainian Nationalists (OUN) had won out. It was led by a hot-headed Galician named Stepan Bandera.

Founded in the aftermath of the failure to form an enduring independent Ukrainian state during World War I, and reflecting years of frustration with repressive policies against Ukrainians, OUN embraced violence and terrorism as legitimate forms of political action. It was responsible for a number of assassinations, attacks, and incidents of arson in the interwar years, principally against representations of Polish power. As World War II dawned, scrambling Europe's borders, OUN saw greater opportunity for Ukrainian autonomy and its ranks swelled.

As the war dragged on, OUN and another nationalist organization fielded their own guerilla fighters in western Ukraine. UPA was born of these efforts; it would deploy tens of thousands of men in its mission to establish an independent Ukrainian state. (While UPA was most closely affiliated with the Bandera faction of OUN and for long stretches essentially run by it, it also acted independently at times.)

The nationalists were realistic. They knew they needed to have the sponsorship of one of the major warring powers to stand a chance of forming and sustaining an independent state, and the

Germans were more likely to support such an undertaking than the Russians. Throughout most of the German occupation, some parts of OUN attempted to make common cause with the Nazis to bring its vision of an independent state into being.

They did not have much success. The Nazis demonstrated lukewarm support for the movement, sending funds to nationalist leaders as late as 1944. They paired that, though, with the persecution of nationalists on the ground. Within weeks of invading Ukraine in 1941, the Germans arrested Bandera. During the three years of occupation that followed, the Nazis imprisoned thousands of suspected Ukrainian nationalists in concentration camps. For this and other reasons, many nationalists thought of the Nazis as enemies.

The nationalists had a more vexing foe, though, in the Soviets. They were also an old, known one: Russia's westward reach had troubled its neighbors for centuries. And while the Nazis viewed Ukrainian nationalism as a nuisance, the Soviets saw it as an existential threat to their vision of their postwar empire. Like Belarusians, Estonians, and scores of other minorities that yearned for autonomy, the Ukrainians had to be brought into line, their culture, traditions, and language managed carefully. A broader Soviet identity had to be forged — and if not forged, then imposed.

The Soviet reconquest of western Ukraine in 1944 dealt the dream of Ukrainian independence a hard blow. In Staryava, the Soviets closed down Mykhailo's beloved Ukrainian cultural club, Prosvita, and boarded up the church of St. Paraskeva, which had earned a reputation as a meeting ground for Ukrainian nationalists. (The priest had gone west with the Germans.) They pumped out propaganda in schools, journals, and cinemas that heroized Soviet forces and demonized the nationalists as "traitors," "fascists," and "enemies of the people." Eager to ferret out nationalists, Soviet agents would show up unannounced at people's houses and subject them to searches, pulling drawers out of bureaus and heaping their contents onto the ground, showing no respect as they ripped through birth certificates, newspapers, wedding photos, report cards. The purpose of these searches, it seems, was as much to flaunt their power and impunity as to find something incriminating.

The tactics the Soviets used were familiar from the first round of occupation from 1939 to 1941, but now the resources devoted to ferreting out nationalists were greater. The Soviets dispatched "destruction battalions" to patrol areas rife with nationalists, and augmented these forces with neighborhood watch groups, outfits that were ragtag and prone to violent behavior. They were quick to see in any western Ukrainian a nationalist sympathizer—or brand a person as one if it could excuse violence.

Initially, the Soviets allowed the UPA fighters they killed to be buried in the village cemetery and afforded a proper funeral, but after they saw how many mourners turned out, they barred the practice. The Soviets took to burying bodies in random places or leaving them on public display as a warning. For days, the corpses of two of my grandmother's schoolmates who had been killed fighting for UPA lay in the green the villagers used as a soccer field. One afternoon, while Stefania Midyanka's father was plowing his garden, he stumbled on a man's freshly-buried body. He found another a few feet away. He reported his discovery to a Soviet official in the village, who told him not to worry because the men they killed, the nationalists, were worse than dogs.

Even people who sidestepped the Soviets' scrutiny had to contend with major changes to daily life. The Soviets moved forward with collectivization, destabilizing the delicate arrangements that allowed most peasants to generate a modest livelihood through small-scale farming. And they instituted a draft. When the Red Army retook eastern Galicia in 1944, it was hemorrhaging soldiers, and it desperately needed men who could fight. They also wanted to prevent young men from joining the nationalists.

Even if a Ukrainian man was ideologically receptive to fighting for the Soviet army, he had to understand that enlisting was likely tantamount to signing a death sentence. Faced with this horrible choice, Ukrainian men went to the forests in droves to join the nationalists.

I absorbed these facts viscerally as I went through the case files on my great-grandfather Mykhailo's brothers, which I had received by email from an archive before my trip. The files had been scanned carefully and sent as high-resolution images. Their quality was so good that I could make out the gradients of blue in the handwriting and the rivulets inside the thumbprints that sat at the bottom of some of the pages, in lieu of a photograph or signature. In some places, I could see that the police had underlined in pencil phrases that they found especially helpful, tokens of information they used to build their cases against the brothers.

Both men had joined UPA and were captured by the NKVD, the Soviet secret police, in separate operations within 16 months of the Soviets' reoccupation of western Ukraine in the summer of 1944.

The first file I read through belonged to yet another Stepan Mazur. He was eleven years younger than his brother, my great-grandfather Mykhailo. By the time the war started, Stepan and his wife had three boys, the eldest of whom was my grandmother's cousin Slavik, the mischievous former bicyclist who now lived near my aunt Stefa. According to the file, Stepan's holdings were humble — the only significant livestock on his small farm in Staryava was a cow. Throughout the German occupation, he supported his family by working the land and taking gigs at the timber factory.

When the Soviets recaptured western Ukraine in the summer of 1944, thirty-seven-year-old Stepan received a draft notice from the Red Army. He tried to dodge conscription by hiding in his father's house. He managed to do so until May 1945, when he sought refuge in the nearby forest instead. Presumably he joined UPA at that time. In January 1946, he was captured in the forest along with four other suspected UPA combatants.

To Stepan's misfortune, when he was arrested, he had a gun.

Stepan's case file contains transcripts of four interrogations by Soviet police following his arrest. These records offer a portrait of a man at times defiant, at times resigned. Recorded by hand, they must have been only an approximation of what occurred. And NKVD files, like the files of any totalitarian regime, should be treated with skepticism — the Soviet Union had a long history of obtaining false confessions and manipulating legal documents. Surely the files could have been altered to meet the needs of the regime; surely the subjects of the files would have many reasons to lie to their interrogators. And there is no mention of the torture that was known to accompany interrogations and influence their outcomes.

Yet, the documents are what I had.

"Your weaponry. What was the goal of keeping it on you?" the Soviet official asks Stepan in the first interrogation.

"I found the weaponry in the forest and kept it on myself," Stepan says.

"Are you being honest?"

"I never killed anyone with this gun. I'm telling the truth."

"Was there anyone who was leading your gang?"

"There was no head person in my gang."

"You're not telling the truth. Be honest."

Stepan's denials continue: "Honestly, there was no head person." "I swear I don't know who was hiding where." "I am not a nationalist. I was afraid of the threat of the Soviet regime and I was hiding from it, and that was it."

In the second interrogation, the authorities are still trying to get him to provide more details about the gun.

"You could have hidden without the guns and arms. But you had weapons for fighting," the interrogator points out.

"Yes, I had guns to fight the Soviet Army. But I didn't use them."

"You're lying," the interrogator retorts. "Tell me exactly what kind of armed battle you did with the Soviet regime."

"I swear, I didn't fight them at all."

The questions continue in this vein, until the third interrogation, when Stepan admits his guilt without protest. "Yes, I am completely guilty," he says after the interrogator reads the charges against him. He states for the record that he was in UPA and that he did have a pseudonym and a gun.

"What can you add to your answers?" the interrogator asks.

"Nothing," Stepan says. "The protocol looks right to me."

By late March 1946, Stepan had been sentenced to ten years in a gulag labor camp and five additional years of internal exile. While he was in the camp, his wife and three young boys were deported to Yemanzehlinsk as part of Operation West. Stepan survived his time in the labor camp and eventually joined them there.

The second file, on Stepan and Mykhailo's younger brother Andriy, showed that he had a different trajectory. By the time he was fifteen, both of his parents had died so he had to make do with even less than what his older siblings had had growing up. In his interrogation, Andriy reports that he only had two years of schooling before he turned to full-time work in the fields. By the end of the war, most of his brothers and sisters had embarked on lives of their own. He lived in his late father's house with Nastka, his younger sister by four years.

Andriy tells his interrogators that he was brought into the nationalist fray by a few men from Staryava; a family friend had visited him in January 1945 and tried to convince him to join, arguing he would soon be forced into the Red Army. Andriy contended that he was too young to be drafted, but when two UPA soldiers visited him in March of that year and pressed the point, he relented and joined them in the forest.

Andriy was captured during a shootout with border police in April 1945. He was seventeen years old at the time. He had been in UPA about a month.

Andriy is less combative in the two transcribed interrogations than his brother had been, and more forthcoming with specific and incriminating information. A teenager, he was probably scared out of his wits. The group he was part of had five weapons, he tells his interrogator. Ten to twenty bullets. Four grenades. He admits his gun had been taken away during the clash with the border police, His main role in the group was to keep watch at night.

The price he paid was considerable. For Andriy's month in UPA, he was sentenced to ten years in a gulag labor camp.

10
"Unreliable"

One afternoon about two weeks after I returned to the U.S., my phone started convulsing with a series of chimes. They were texts from Lida in Lviv. Her request for access to the files on our family's exile had been approved, and she had gone to the Ministry of Internal Affairs to view them that day. Altogether, the ministry had 147 pages relating to the exile of my family to Siberia, organized in four separate files for each of the adults who had been deported: my grandmother; my grandfather; my great-grandmother Rozalia; and Ivan, my grandmother's brother. Stefa, who was only six years old at the time of the deportation, did not have a file.

Lida had photocopied each of the 147 pages. When the official turned her back, she snuck a few photos of the pages with her phone and sent those, too.

Later that evening, I transferred the materials Lida had texted me to my computer and started to read through them. Each file had a cover folder that identified it in mimeographed pink ink as the personal file of a special settler, along with a note that the subject was a family member of a Ukrainian nationalist. In the upper-right-hand corner, an official had used pencil to cross out the pink word "secret."

Exile as a political tool has long had special resonance in Russia, first appearing in tsarist law in the mid-seventeenth century. It became a primary instrument of governance only in Stalin's time, when the system of forced labor camps in Siberia was officially designated the gulag. Special settlements were incorporated into the gulag circa 1930, when a senior Soviet official introduced the idea of creating "colonization villages" in the vast parts of Soviet territory that were rich in natural resources like coal, iron, and timber but unfriendly to human habitation. These resources had been envisioned as the fuel for the industrialization prescribed in Stalin's first Five-Year Plan, launched in 1928, under which the Soviet government sought to rapidly modernize what had been a largely agrarian country. Deporting kulaks — middle-class peasants thought to be resistant to collectivization — was a way to kill two birds with one stone. Kulaks from across the Soviet Union were uprooted from their homes to serve as the first inhabitants of these special settlements; in many cases, they arrived to nothing but a blank swath of taiga. It was common for people to die during the difficult trip east or in the effort to provide themselves with shelter in the harsh environment. "The deportees suffered just as much as their countrymen who had been sent to labor camps, if not more so," wrote the gulag historian Anne Applebaum. "At least those in camps had a daily bread ration and a place to sleep. Exiles often had neither."

While deportations to special settlements waned in the mid-1930s, the Soviets continued to use them as a means to both political and economic ends. During the war, deportation became a favored tool of Stalin for disarming groups that posed real or imagined threats to Soviet power. Germans, Poles, Jews, Czechs, Lithuanians, Latvians, Estonians, Greeks, Hungarians, Crimean Tatars, Chechens, and a host of ethnic groups inside Russia were sent from their homes to gulag exile settlements.

The Soviets had already deported thousands of Ukrainian nationalists and their family members by the time they sanctioned the operation that took my family. The Mazurs knew the danger intimately: Rozalia's younger brother had been a member of UPA and sometime during the war, her mother, Yulia, had been exiled to Arkhangelsk, in subarctic Russia, as a result. Within a year, the letters and packages her distraught family sent her came back unopened. From this, they understood that she had died.

The operation that targeted my grandparents was different from the ones that preceded it. "In our work, there is one mistake," an official argued at a conference for Soviet secret police agents in Lviv Oblast in 1945. "We kill rebels, we see the rebel lying dead, but each rebel leaves behind a wife, a brother, a sister, and so on." For Operation West, the Soviets explicitly sought to apprehend family members of suspected UPA soldiers en masse. They wanted to critically weaken the rebels' source of support.

The Soviets planned the operation down to the smallest detail: the people they planned to exile; the secret police and intelligence officers who would staff the operation; the railway cars, horse-drawn wagons, and transportation routes they would use to ferry the arrested people east. A week before the operation, on October 15, the Council of Ministers of the USSR adopted a resolution permitting the state to appropriate the property of families after they were deported. There would be no appeal, no recourse, no trial to adjudicate the decision that the deported were *nenadezhni* — unreliable.

On the morning of October 21, residents of Lviv were taken away as early as two a.m., while people living in rural areas were apprehended beginning at six a.m. It was cold — in some parts of Ukraine, the operation was hindered by snowfall. The nationalists had gotten word that the deportation was imminent, so some people who thought they would be taken gathered food and clothing to bring. My family members were in denial about whether they would be targeted, and so when the police arrived, they did what desperate people often do: They ran. My grandmother and Rozalia rushed six-year-old Stefa to the fields and crouched amid the tall grass, but someone gave them away. Rozalia tried to get her granddaughter to flee as the police approached but Stefa clung to her skirts. The police pushed them all into the horse-drawn wagons with only the clothes on their backs.

Ivan hid in a neighbor's attic but he too was turned in. "Look, look, they're here!" cried the person who discovered him. When the Soviet police got their hands on the nineteen-year-old Ivan, they beat him, and he boarded the horse-drawn wagon with blood flowing from his head. My grandfather had risen early that morning to work in the fields, as usual, but somehow the police found him and arrested him, too. Family photos, clothing, valuables, official documents, Mike's address in the United States — they had no choice but to leave it all behind.

The wagons took them to Khyriv, about five miles down the road, where they were transferred from wagons to cattle cars. More than eighteen hundred people were deposited in Khyriv for this purpose. Pulling forty cattle cars packed with up to forty-five people each, the train then started in its plodding trip east. Altogether, more than seventy-six thousand Ukrainians would be deported as part of the operation.

The journey in the cattle cars was grueling. The passengers would be let out for an hour every day or so to gather water; sometimes the authorities would give them soup. The passengers would call out to people walking along the railroad tracks and ask where they were. "Everything happened on those trains — birth, death, everything," Slavik, my grandmother's cousin, told me. Soviet records report that 875 deportees tried to escape the trains, though they also claim that the able Soviet security force recaptured the majority — 515.

The longer the trains rolled on, the fewer responses the captured passengers got in Ukrainian, until all they were hearing was Russian, which they didn't understand well, and names of towns that were distantly familiar or that they didn't recognize at all.

The files Lida retrieved had details that had faded from the memories of those I had spoken with. Some of these details were small, banal even, but they made the picture of my family's exile clearer.

They gave me a date — November 4, 1947, two weeks after my family was arrested — for when their journey ended and they were formally registered in Siberia.

I knew from interviewing my grandmother that within ten days of arriving, my grandparents and Ivan had been recast from farmers who worked the land to miners who toiled beneath it. (Rozalia, then aged forty-five, was deemed too old for work.) I knew that in her first days underground my grandmother had been wracked with anxiety as she navigated the narrow, dark tunnels by the light on her headlamp. I knew that one of her early worries was that she would not be able to find her way out of the mine, and that she learned to observe the water running along the sides of the tunnels because they naturally flowed toward an exit. From the files, I learned that her mine had a number — 18 — and that Ivan and my grandfather were assigned to work there, too.

I knew that my grandparents had been assigned to barracks where three to four families shared one room, and I learned from the files that it was barrack 3, apartment 13. I knew from my grandmother that they lived essentially under house arrest, especially those first few years. "If I had to go to work in the morning, I had to stop by the chief's barracks. If I went to the market, I had to go and say, 'I am going to the market for an hour or two," she had told me. They had to formally report to the commander to demonstrate that they were still physically present, and I found it extraordinary that the files contained the sheets of paper on which the commander instructed them to sign their surnames twice a month.

Even more extraordinary was that Ivan's file contained his sign-in sheets from 1951, the year he was arrested and sent deeper into the gulag system, to a formal labor camp. My grandmother had recounted to me the anguish the family felt when he disappeared . one day. His wife was pregnant with their first child; Ivan was twenty-three years old. The only thing the settlement authorities would tell the family was that he was not in the mine because they could account for the token that he was required to wear around his neck while he was on the premises.

My grandmother had recounted that the family was only able to confirm that Ivan was in a prison in Chelyabinsk, a city about thirty-five miles north of Yemanzhelinsk. They learned this from a woman who had voluntarily moved from Ukraine to Yemanzhelinsk to live with her boyfriend. Because the woman could travel relatively freely, the family asked her to go to town and make inquiries.

The sign-in sheets in Ivan's file go blank starting in September 1951.

Ivan's file also contained six pages detailing the case against him that caused his disappearance. He and eight other young Ukrainian men had been arrested in late August, accused of organizing gatherings where songs glorifying UPA were sung. Some of the men were charged with trying to aid UPA directly. At one of these suspicious parties, Ivan had allegedly given a toast in honor of UPA and all those repressed under the Soviet regime. The authorities noted a second instance, in the summer of 1950, when, using methods unstated, Ivan "slandered the Soviet regime."

The file shows that Ivan was tried, found guilty, and sentenced in January 1952. That March, he was transferred to the notorious Ozerlag labor camp in Irkutsk Oblast, more than two thousand miles east of Yemanzhelinsk. The occupations in the Ozerlag varied—some prisoners worked in mines; others logged the abundant larch, pine, and birch of the region's forests; still others toiled in railroad construction. Prisoners were able to send and receive mail, and Ivan wrote to his family about the terrible snow in the winters and the hordes of mosquitoes in the summer. Back in Yemanzhelinsk, the family scraped together what they could and sent it to him so that he could barter for a net to shield his face from bugs.

There is no record of Ivan's punishment being reduced during the "thaw" in Soviet repression that followed the death of Stalin in 1953. Just five years into a twenty-five-year sentence, Ivan was freed and returned to his family in Yemanzhelinsk, though he would remain a lesser citizen in the eyes of the Soviet regime until its demise.

There were more details about my family's experience in Siberia that the files did not contain, that I knew only because my grandmother had spoken about them in my recorded conversations with her. There is no evidence of the guidance my grandmother received — and ignored — to put Stefa in a state orphanage because she would be busy working in the mine. "We were told, 'Ah, your child will be at the daycare. It's better there.' Who knew where that daycare was? We could not even freely go to the market!" she had told me. "If they took her, I didn't know whether we would ever find her, because they changed the names of the children. If a child was older and remembered who her parents were, she could find them, but if the child could not remember and she was told that she is, let's say Marusia or Sonia or whoever, then that child would grow up without knowing who she really was."

There were no details about the number of wells in the settlement that contained potable water — very few — or about the fights that would break out over access to them as the barracks residents queued beside them with their poles and water buckets.

There was no mention in the files of the fleas that infested the barracks or the malaria that tormented the deportees like a scourge. "I had malaria for maybe two or three years," my grandmother told me. "Malaria, that's when you are healthy — "

"I know what it is," I said.

"No, you don't," she said. "You are healthy and then one minute you feel cold. The next you are hot, hot, hot." She grimaced. "Then you do not feel well at all. Then you are cold again. You freeze and shake. They can put ten blankets on you and they don't help. When the fever's gone, you can go to the hospital, but by then you are healthy. You're not sick at all. Then it starts again. That's what it is."

There was no indication in the files that the walk from the barracks to the mines took an hour, and longer in the winter when the snow and wind were at their Siberian height. There was no documentation that after a miner completed her shift and the long walk back to her barracks, the next thing she would often do would be to go back out into the night and stand in the queue that offered her family the only chance to procure a loaf of bread. There was no record that sometimes the waiting would be in vain, because even though as a miner she was entitled to a kilogram of bread and three hundred grams for her child, sometimes the bureaucrat in charge only had enough bread for those at the beginning of the line.

"It was a terrible regime," she said. "When people in Ukraine say they long for Soviet times, it shakes me all up. I say even now, 'Did you forget how [in Siberia] you had to wait in the line to buy bread, how a person had to come after the second shift at one or two in the morning to wait at the store?' You would be in line to buy bread for the next day and you would write the number of your place in line on your hand. But then they would say *fizicheskaya ochered* – physical queue – at the shop. Do you know what a physical queue is?"

I shook my head.

"There could be around a hundred people in line. When the bread was close to being delivered, the store opened and then someone would shout *fizicheskaya ochered!* That meant the line and the numbers wouldn't be accepted. The only thing that mattered was where you were standing. A few people would buy and then – no bread!"

The files contained no trace of the times my grandmother was transferred from the mines to potato fields where she ran a tractor during the harvest and how the authorities arrested workers who were caught stuffing mauled, rotten potatoes in their clothes out of hunger because even these remnants were "state's property." "If you took the potato and hid it and ran away with it, it wouldn't get rotten. You had to steal them," she said. "They taught people how to steal." Indignation rang in her voice.

There is no indication that the Soviet authorities took the same view of the wood chips that were the byproducts of construction in the settlement, or that they knew that deportees, including my grandmother, crept outside at night to steal them because they literally had nothing to burn, and that without the warmth of a fire, it got so cold in the barracks that the water would freeze at night. There is no signal that the Soviets knew of the scheme my grandmother and others orchestrated to distract the guards at a coal station near the barracks, so that they could steal coal to generate the heat for which they were desperate.

There is no list of the responsibilities my grandmother had at the mine over the nearly twenty years she worked there, from carrying up to twenty-five pounds of explosives from the staging point to the mine three kilometers away; to drilling the explosives into the wall; to bracing herself for the explosion and then shoveling the ore shards from the freshly crumbled wall into a wagon; to being a part of a group that used their shoulders to push the wagon holding up to a ton of ore toward an electric train that would convey the wagon out of the mine.

There is no record of a saying the Soviet authorities would recite when a mine caved in and crushed those working in it. Because there would now be a smaller payroll, "the spoons will be cheaper."

"Often, when someone asks me about it, I say that it is better not to say anything because when I talk about it, I think I will forget it, but then I think about it all night long," she told me. "It's difficult. You can think, your family is here, your kids are here, but when mine were growing up there was no bread. Milk cost ten rubles per liter. One liter was not enough. In the mine, we made twenty-five rubles a day as women. How is that a life?"

11
Thorough and Brutal

Stefan, my grandmother's brother, had his name all over the exile files. He was cited again and again as the reason the Mazurs were sent to Siberia.

Few of the details were new but they were powerful. The first was that Stefan had died in battle with Soviet forces on November 25, 1946. No one in my family had known the date of Stefan's death. When I saw it, my impulse was to share the news with my grandmother, though of course she was not there to hear it.

Another detail was that Stefan's UPA pseudonym was *Krit* — "Mole." The men in the woods assumed pseudonyms to reduce the risk to themselves and their families. It would have been completely understandable if this detail did not match with any of the others I had heard. How many times had I come across information that confused rather than clarified? But the pseudonym did match. One of the entries in the directory of UPA members compiled by Zenon Shandrovich indicated that "Mole" was the pseudonym of the Stefan Mazur from Staryava who had served in the Ukrainian auxiliary police under the Nazis. Just like the man in the photo on the Yad Vashem website.

The correlation vexed me, but I couldn't think of any more avenues to confirm my suspicions. My queries to Yad Vashem, the Holocaust remembrance center in Jerusalem, had revealed only that the staff there thought the file had come from somewhere in Eastern Europe, and every inquiry I sent to a Ukrainian archive on the matter yielded nothing.

I should have known by that point that institutions that once operated behind the Iron Curtain were still prone to working at a pace, and with a logic, all their own. One ordinary day, while I was waiting to catch a bus to work, I got an email from a Ukrainian archivist I had contacted years earlier. Stefan's name was in the subject line.

Attached to the email was a high-quality version of the image of the Ukrainian policeman that had appeared on the Yad Vashem website. (By that point, the museum had taken down the image and its headline, "Stefan Masur, a Ukrainian war criminal," for reasons unknown.) The photo was part of a relatively mundane document, a man's single-page application to join the Ukrainian police in 1942. It was not mundane to me, though. My heart beating fast, I looked carefully at the information on the application: the man's birth date, his place of birth, his next of kin. The man had applied to join the police on April 15, around the time Stefan was recorded as being absent from Germany. All of it matched what I knew of Stefan.

The photo was sharper and clearer than the photocopied version that had appeared on the Yad Vashem website. The man's face was squarer than it had seemed online. His irises looked lighter — would they be described as gray? My knees went weak as I realized that the man resembled Rozalia Mazur. His mother.

There was no doubt about it: the man in the photo — the "Ukrainian war criminal" — was Stefan, my grandmother's brother.

After staring at the document for a while, I closed it on my phone and looked out at the passing traffic. A number of feelings coursed through me. A desire to share the photo with my grandmother, who had so few photos of the brother she loved. Satisfaction at answering a question I had been circling for so long. But over both of these emotions hung dread — dread at the thought of what Stefan must have done as a policeman.

Vivid scenes played out in my mind: Stefan's young face among the Ukrainians enthusiastically offering the Nazi salute to their new rulers at the rally in Dobromil in the first days of the German occupation in 1941. Stefan herding the Jews into lines as they awaited evacuation to the Belzec extermination camp, or shooting at them as they cowered in their hiding spots in an evacuated ghetto, or turning in families that had attempted to find refuge in the forest — all roles the Ukrainian police played in support of the Final Solution. I considered that when a Jewish Holocaust survivor was warned not to return to his native village near Staryava when the war ended because the Ukrainians might kill him, Stefan may have been one of the young men willing to pull the trigger.

As I processed these thoughts over the next days and weeks, another familiar feeling emerged: curiosity. It turned out that the reason that the file had been so hard to get was because it was in Poland, not Ukraine. In the European Union, archival restrictions were more stringent. My archival contact suggested that I use the police application to query the Polish archive for additional files it might hold about Stefan and learn more about what he had done as a member of the Ukrainian police. Unlike in Ukraine, it would not be so straightforward as simply sending an email. No Polish archival officials would be friending me on Facebook.

Thankfully, by that point, I had plenty of help to draw on. An affable, Polish-speaking librarian at the Holocaust Memorial Museum in D.C. worked with me on my request to the Polish government to view additional files about Stefan. "You have to be strategic," he told me cheerfully as he typed. "Play to their politics and their heart strings." "KILLED DURING THE SO-CALLED SOVIET 'LIBERATION' IN 1946," he wrote in Polish in a section inviting biographical background about Stefan. ("All caps is good," he said. "Makes you seem less savvy, more pitiable.") "MY GRAND-MOTHER NEVER KNEW WHERE HE WAS BURIED," he typed. "SHE DIED WITHOUT KNOWING WHAT THOSE COM-MUNISTS DID TO HER BROTHER."

It took six months for the archive to review — and reject — my request. Apparently, Polish law required that only the living family member closest to the subject could be granted access to personal documents. So I redid the application with my mother as the applicant. ("MY MOTHER NEVER KNEW WHERE HE WAS BUR-IED...") Months passed before we heard that my mother's application had passed muster and she was welcome to view the file at her convenience at an archive in a town in southeastern Poland called Rzeszow, where it was located.

Needless to say, my mother did not find it at all convenient to visit Rzeszow, so I hired a Polish archival researcher to make a trip and copy the files. We had to produce a power of attorney document in Polish to authorize him to perform the task. It seemed like yet another difficult proposition but thankfully the guy in Cleveland who had handled the packages my grandmother sent to Ukraine for decades was also well-versed in the diverse logistical realms in which Ukrainians in the United States needed help when trying to navigate the bureaucracy in their home country. Even better, he was authorized as a notary in Ukraine and several adjacent countries, including Poland. He happily signed off on the document I cobbled together with the help of the Internet. Winking at me, he put a few extra stamps on the signatory page, knowing that stamps held an almost comic authority with Eastern European bureaucrats.

A few weeks later, I sat once again in front of my computer opening an email that would reveal another buried aspect of my family's experience during the war. I held my breath and clicked on the first file. The screen blinked and then resolved into an image of a pale green file folder. The title of the file read KOLABORANT.

I didn't have to know any Polish to know what that meant.

With the help of an online translator, I quickly understood that the file was an artifact of a series of investigations the Polish Ministry of Interior undertook to prosecute claims of police brutality against Polish citizens during the Nazi occupation. "KOLABORANT," or collaborator, turned out to be the name of the case, which considered the activities of six Ukrainian auxiliary policemen who operated in a cluster of small towns and villages in southeastern Poland during the war. Stefan was one of them.

In the file, he was cited for an incident involving a man named Andrzej Martyniak. In January 1943, Andrzej was in his mid-twenties, just a few years older than the twenty-year-old Stefan. Stefan and another policeman arrested Andrzej in a village called Wyszatyce; six other men were arrested at the same time, though it's unclear if Stefan was involved. In his written statement, Andrzej didn't explain the reason for his arrest, but it was likely for a minor legal violation akin to what caused the downfall of my grandmother's first husband, Yosip Punko. The arrested men were likely either Polish or Ukrainian, as none had Jewish names.

Andrzej and his cohort were imprisoned at a jail in Przemysl for about six weeks. Then they were ordered into cattle cars bound for Auschwitz. Andrzej and three other men escaped from the moving train, and Andrzej made his way back to his farm. A few weeks later, while walking around at home, he saw Stefan and another policeman approaching his house. He fled in the direction of the barn but they caught sight of him and ran after him. Stefan fired three shots at Andrzej, striking him in the leg and causing him to fall to the ground.

Andrzej was taken to the hospital to be treated. As soon as he had healed enough, he escaped again. He made his way home and the scene repeated itself: Stefan and another policeman came round and captured him. This time, he was roughed up and sent to jail. Again he managed to escape. Now, Andrzej knew better than to return home and instead joined the partisans in the forest. It proved a wise choice, as Andrzej survived the war.

A different witness also named Stefan as one of two men who had killed a Soviet officer, but there is no corroborating information about that accusation.

Reading the file, I was a bit underwhelmed (though impressed by Andrzej's tenacity). This was it? Stefan had shot someone in the leg who had escaped policy custody? In the United States, you might not even lose your job in those circumstances if you were a policeman, much less spark an investigation by a national agency (not that the U.S. is the exemplar of policing). Given that scenes of abject barbarity had played out on a daily basis in wartime Poland,

I was surprised to see that the prosecution didn't have higher priorities.

Likely it did: The case was closed within a year of being opened in 1965. Most of the men under investigation did not live on Polish territory, an official noted, and efforts to receive additional information about their whereabouts abroad were unsuccessful.

Regardless, the file did show that, as I suspected, Stefan had played one of the critical roles the Ukrainian police during the Holocaust: arresting people and sending them to concentration camps. The file showed that he did this faithfully and repeatedly. How many times had he marched someone onto a train bound for Auschwitz or Sobibor? How many people had he hunted?

The file did not contain the answers to these questions.

And then I thought of my grandmother, and her love for her older brother, and I felt helpless before the complexity of life.

Just as unexpectedly as the archivist's email had appeared, so too did a note from the Ministry of Internal Affairs in Lviv. It turned out that it also possessed a file on Stefan. Never mind that I had queried the ministry years earlier on just this very matter and gotten a negative response. I had long ago accepted that my knowledge would always be partial and the result of luck as much as effort.

The archive's protocols must have changed, because this time Lida did not need to go to the ministry and photocopy the documents. The ministry was able to send it to me by email. The file concerned Stefan's activities as part of a group of UPA combatants active near Staryava. It was here that my research took an even darker turn.

Before I started to research my family's history in depth, I knew that their greatest political allegiance during the war was to Ukraine. What they wanted most of all was for it to become an independent country. For them, this was not an intellectual exercise. It was a commitment born of lived experience and inherited history—of the many years in which they and their forebears were forced to attend school in another language, barred from celebrating their culture fully, denied political representation, kept from holding many kinds of jobs, and saddled with a grinding poverty that seemed to (but did not actually) afflict the Ukrainians most of all.

Stefan's commitment to Ukrainian nationalism had been seeded in his youth, when he frequented Prosvita, the Ukrainian cultural club whose local branch his father had helped found. Several men in the club were secretly members of the OUN faction led by Stepan Bandera, and they had their eyes peeled for trustworthy young people to recruit to their cause. "I immediately went numb," a woman Stefan's age recounted when recalling the moment when she, a girl of sixteen, was invited by a widely respected Prosvita member in Staryava to join the youth branch of OUN. The man had been "courting" her for a while, giving her books to read and talking about them with her at length. "I was so pleased. I trusted and respected him greatly. I couldn't believe that someone would ever make me an offer like that." After recovering from her shock, she accepted the man's invitation. "I did not walk home, I flew. I wanted to tell everyone but I immediately remembered the instructions: don't tell anyone about it, even the people closest to you."

OUN propaganda portrayed its adherents as honest, brave, and prudent, qualities that would have appealed to an earnest young man like Stefan. Men in the forest celebrated religious holidays like Easter. They recited prayers before meals, and hung crosses on the dirt walls of their underground bunkers. "Know that God is best honored through the Nation and in the name of the Nation by active love for Ukraine and by the strict morals of the fighter," OUN instructed in materials for new members.

Stefan's service in the Ukrainian auxiliary police could have even stemmed from his allegiance to the movement: Ukrainian nationalists eager to see it develop a military arm encouraged patriotic Ukrainian men to join Nazi forces to gain experience and weapons. Once the nationalists had established their own military force, UPA instructed the policemen to abandon the service and join up.

By the summer of 1943, UPA had extended into eastern Galicia after getting its start in the nearby region of Volhynia.

By the summer of 1944, Stefan had left policework and returned to Staryava. My grandmother finally had her brother back. She was nineteen, the mother of a three-year-old, and a veteran of living in the midst of war. She would have realized that any misstep could have fatal consequences, that even in the safest, most familiar places you could be stalked by an unseen threat.

My guess is that she did not push Stefan for information about how he had spent his time away, and that he knew enough to keep it from her. They both understood by then the safety of ignorance.

In any case, no sooner had Stefan come back than he was gone again, off to the woods as a member of the nationalist underground. "I'm going to stay here with the boys," he told his sister, "to do what needs to be done."

The Soviet authorities had caught wind of Stefan's activities. Officials would arrive unannounced at the Mazur farm and demand to know where he was. The family offered up all manner of lies: The Germans had taken him when they retreated. No, no, they hadn't seen him. At one point, the Soviets arrested Rozalia, brought her to Khryiv, and interrogated her for days. Accounts from other women suggest that torture and rape occurred in these settings; perhaps she endured that, too.

Whatever transpired, Rozalia didn't reveal her son's whereabouts. The cardinal rule of the family was to keep quiet.

The Mazurs did more than obfuscate. As the Soviet secret police force that would later exile them suspected, they fed, sheltered, and assisted the young men who had joined the nationalist cause. In their house, under the floorboards, they had a *kriyivka*, a dirt pit that could conceal nationalist fighters. At night, my grandmother would crawl through the high grass of her family's fields to reach the forest where her brother and his fellow combatants hid. She brought food — bread and milk, and eggs and meat when they had them — and left it in a place where they would find it. My grandmother also acted as a night watch, and masked her warnings in imitations of a bird call, a cat's meow, or a dog's bark if she saw something suspicious. At least once, after dark, she helped carry the corpses of UPA combatants from a nearby border checkpoint to Staryava so their families could bury them. If my grandmother hadn't had a young daughter, she may very well have gone to the forest as a combatant herself, as a number of women did.

I'm very glad she didn't. Like other nationalist movements in Europe at the time, OUN twisted its adherents' instinct for righteousness by making violence and self-sacrifice the epitome of right action. To give oneself to the nationalist cause was a glorious form of martyrdom. "In order for the nation to live, its best sons must die," read one UPA circular.

In keeping with the notion of nation above all, combatants were expected to commit suicide if they suspected that their opponents were on the verge of capturing them. "Neither entreaties, nor threats, nor torture, nor death will force me to betray secrets," went one commandment included in a handbook for soldiers. Time and time again, they followed through. "*Ukrainian guerillas fought with a resolution that no resistance in western Europe could have imagined,*" wrote one historian (emphasis mine).

The movement was ruthless in other ways. The nationalists' overtures to the Nazis were motivated by more than just political convenience. There were key ideological similarities between the nationalists' governing philosophy and that of the Nazis. Much like other radical nationalist groups in Europe at the time, OUN sought to establish an ethnically-pure state—a "Ukraine for Ukrainians" and not Poles, Russians, or Jews. Its leaders admired Hitler, Mussolini, and their kind, and grafted the trappings of their movements, like the one-handed salute, onto the Ukrainian cause. Greatly influenced by nationalist ideologue Dmytro Dontsov, who propagated the idea of a racially pure country, the nationalists had as a foundational text a Decalogue that prescribed extreme positions—for example, that Ukrainians should only marry other Ukrainians because otherwise your "children will become your enemy."

On the eve of the German attack on the Soviet Union in June 1941, for instance, Bandera and other senior OUN leaders developed a highly detailed plan for the organization's activities in the war's next, heightened stage. The plan called for the creation of blacklists of prominent Poles, Communists, and Ukrainians with independent politics and established that most Russians, Jews, and Poles should be "neutralized" upon the installation of an OUN-run state. "Our power must be terrible for its opponents," they wrote.

The most gruesome acts keeping with that directive were carried out by OUN's Security Service, the Sluzhba Bezpeky (SB). SB members were of a different ilk than the typical UPA solider. The SB had a number of highly sensitive functions, such as acting as security for the OUN and UPA leadership, assuring the ideological purity and commitment of the rank and file, and managing the logistics of warfare. To be chosen for a role in the SB was something of an honor — it meant that your judgment was trusted.

In practice, though, membership in the SB was a dark privilege. Like the Gestapo and NKVD, the secret police forces on which it was modeled, the SB was an instrument of terror. It targeted all those who resisted the nationalists' will. As the insurgency dragged on, that even included SB members' compatriots — Ukrainians who refused to join or support UPA — and UPA fighters who failed to toe the movement's rigid line. "The war after the war — my god!" Stefania Midyanka told me, remembering the violence that roiled western Ukraine in what was ostensibly peacetime.

"They didn't choose people to join the SB because they were well-read; what mattered was that they were thorough and brutal," one former SB leader admitted. These qualities, in fact, were encouraged: A slogan taught to new SB members was "Don't think too long, just act."

Anonymous accusations of informing on UPA combatants or fraternizing with the Red Army were all it took for a peasant to receive a death sentence from the SB. The SB usually performed the most vicious killings, and its methods were just as terrible as those practiced by Soviet and Nazi forces. The SB's unluckiest victims could be stripped naked and strung up on a noose, or hacked to pieces. Sometimes SB forces attached threatening messages to the corpses or scrawled them onto structures near the bodies in the blood of the dead. The point was not just to eliminate potential opponents, but to cow those who remained into obeying the nationalists' demands. According to Soviet records, it was estimated that more than two-thirds of the nationalists' victims were civilians.

The nationalists had a vision for governance that was similar to that of the totalitarian regimes they fought against. At the height of UPA insurgency, Stefania Midyanka's sister Hanya was courted by a young man in the village who was a nationalist. Her father put a stop to the relationship because he didn't want the family to be mistaken for supporters of the cause. "Son, do not come here," he told the young man. "I don't want my bones to be buried somewhere because someone said I fought for Ukraine."

The man was enraged. "If it were not for Hanya, I would shoot you right now," he said, his voice dripping with contempt. Like Stefan, the young man went on to die in his early twenties in battle with Soviet forces.

During World War II, when the Germans' fortunes began to fade, OUN and UPA had tried to reform their agenda to win the support of the Americans. In 1943, OUN moderated its platform, adopting a "two-front strategy" that opposed both the Soviets and Nazis and promising "equality to all citizens of Ukraine, whatever their nationality." OUN also removed Jews from the list of enemies its members should purposely seek out and kill (though, by this point, most of the Jews in the areas where it was active were dead.) On the ground, though, the nationalists' methods didn't change much; violence against non-Ukrainians continued. The historian John-Paul Himka estimates that the Jews who survived the Nazi killing sprees and sheltered in the forest or in hiding only to die at the hands of the nationalists numbered in the thousands, if not more. Their suffering "defies description," Himka wrote.

In the Volhynia region north of Lviv, UPA embarked on a campaign to rid the area of Poles, and attempted to replicate this effort in eastern Galicia. "When it comes to the Polish question, this is not a military but a minority question. We will solve it as Hitler solved the Jewish question," wrote a representative of UPA leadership.

The carnage from all of this was vicious, inescapable, and devastating: Hundreds of thousands of people were killed as the nationalists fought various enemies for the sake of establishing an independent, ethnically pure Ukraine.

Back to the files. The documents I received from Ukraine's Ministry of Internal Affairs showed that two men had named Stefan as a member of an UPA group that was behind a series of killings near Staryava in the mid-1940s. The men themselves had been part of the group at one point, and for unclear reasons — torture? a change of heart? participation in one of the amnesties the Soviets offered the nationalists? — had gone from UPA fighters to Soviet informants.

Stefan is the only man in the group identified as an agent of the dreaded SB.

There are no interrogations in the files, no documents punctuated by a black-inked thumbprint. The men simply list the group's activities. They claim that the group had been involved in typical underground work. They killed a handful of Soviet soldiers and border guards. They robbed an oil factory in Khyriv and escaped with a few barrels of fuel. And they executed a number of civilians.

In a few cases, the men specify that the civilians were thought to be helping the Soviets.

In other cases, there is no explanation.

The group killed the director of a school in a village close to Staryava.

They arrested two sisters, Mariya and Kateryna Volchek, and shot them in a forest.

They killed another set of sisters, Rozalia and Klara Nanovska, as well as their mother.

They killed a man named Mykhailo Horno, his wife, and two young children.

The words *war crimes* floated through my mind as I read those sentences.

My effort to trace Stefan's path ended there, as did my research into my family's history. I knew all I wanted — all that I had feared — to know. Yet the end did not feel particularly satisfying. I found myself going back and forth between what I had uncovered about Stefan, how he had been a loving elder brother and a respected member of his community but also a perpetrator of the death of civilians under the banner of ethnic superiority. I wasn't naive — I knew that people's circumstances shaped their behavior and that rural Ukrainian men in Galicia at the time experienced plenty of hardships that, understandably, nudged them toward violence around the time of the war. But it was uncomfortable and vexing to think that Stefan hadn't been able to rise above these difficult circumstances, and to accept that there was such a black mark at the heart of my grandmother's loyalties.

As I tried to make sense of what I had learned about my family's past, I tried to find some wisdom in the present. How were Ukrainians themselves grappling with these difficult chapters of their history?

They had a lot of baggage to work through. Under the Soviet Union, the Kremlin had tightly controlled the narrative about World War II. The version it approved heralded the Red Army for defeating the fascist threat posed by Nazi Germany. In case the Soviet population needed any reminder of its sacrifice, whose 20 million fatalities made the American death toll look miniscule, the government provided it with massive, imposing statues of muscular Soviet heroes from the "Great Patriotic War" and elaborate, red-flagged parades on Victory Day.

In the Kremlin's version of history, Ukrainians who sided with the nationalist movement were no better than the Nazis. Soviet propaganda referred to UPA as "bandits," "the worst enemies of the Ukrainian nation," and "servant[s] of German Fascism," among other condemnations. Ukrainians who were even tangentially associated with the nationalist movement endured scrutiny and discrimination long after the war ended. Shortly after Stefa started a new job in the accounting department of a sanatorium in the 1980s, her managers convened a meeting of the organization and informed the group to be vigilant as a "Ukrainian nationalist is among us" — meaning her.

In independent Ukraine, OUN and UPA obtained a measure of legitimacy that had been absent in the Soviet years. In some parts of the country, namely the west and the center, the forces were applauded, even revered, for the sacrifices they had made for Ukrainian statehood. Some Ukrainians who were subject to exile or gulag camp incarceration because of their affiliation with the nationalist movement, including Stefa and Ivan, were "rehabilitated" and awarded a small pension from the state. (These days, that pension amounts to about $2 a month for Stefa.) In UPA-friendly regions, monuments to Soviet figures were taken down, while tributes to nationalist figures like Stepan Bandera went up. In these areas, you can also find monuments and plaques to Ukrainians who served in the SS Galizien, a Ukrainian division of the German army, with the unit euphemistically referred to as the "First Division of the Ukrainian National Army," as it was rebranded late in the war.

These varied moves were part of a conflict over memory that broadly pitted the western part of country, where Ukrainian nationalism had been widespread during the war, against the eastern part, which had been more Russified and was more sympathetic to the Soviet version of history. In the winter of 2014, the conflict entered a new phase when Ukrainian security forces clashed with demonstrators protesting against the Ukrainian government's abrupt withdrawal from an expected association agreement with the European Union. The clashes left more than one hundred people dead and caused the Ukrainian president, Viktor Yanukovych, to flee the country for Russia. In voting later that year, a Europe-oriented politician, Petro Poroshenko, was elected president. Russia responded to these events by annexing Crimea and occupying parts of Ukraine's eastern flank under the ruse of local separatist movements.

The popularity of OUN and UPA flared on the mixed fuel of the Russian invasion of 2014, the weight of the Yanukovych years, and a new government eager to make its mark. At kiosks and convenience stores in Lviv, small red-and-black UPA flags became ubiquitous. Common OUN sayings like "Glory to Ukraine!" and "Glory to the heroes!" were revived as ways to greet and bid people farewell. Young men, including a set in Staryava, formed UPA reenactment groups and posted their escapades on YouTube. There was little if any acknowledgment of the checkered records of these organizations, no mention of their participation in the Holocaust and mass killing of civilians.

Instead, the new Ukrainian government affirmed the place of the nationalist movement in Ukrainian history. The "decommunization" legislation that was passed in 2015 contained a provision that made it a criminal offense to "show contempt" for those who fought for OUN and UPA. While there have been few prosecutions under the law, it disquieted researchers and specialists working toward a full, unvarnished account of Ukraine's past.

The decommunization policy also targeted the symbols of the former Communist empire. By 2018, more than fifty-two thousand Ukrainian streets had been renamed to remove references to the Soviet past. Every one of the fourteen hundred Lenin statues on the territory under the control of the Ukrainian government was dismantled. Communist Party symbols were pulled from the walls of the Kyiv metro, and the fourth-largest city in Ukraine, Dnipropetrovsk, officially shortened its name to Dnipro to avoid a reference to a former Communist Party leader. "People who are trying to overcome the Soviet legacy are doing it in a very Soviet way," the Ukrainian historian Georgiy Kasianov told me. "In Soviet times, certain things were forbidden. Now, once again, we have this taboo."

If there was something troubling afoot in Ukrainian history, I came to think that it was not in its dark chapters, which can be found in the history of any country. It was in the failure to recognize and account for them, to find a way to tell a story about its past that included them. How could a country know itself unless it knew all the things it had been?

It was a question whose structure was familiar to me. You could ask the same about families.

12

A New Home

In the first years after World War II, the Ukrainian community of Cleveland attempted to facilitate a mass exodus of their compatriots from the smoldering ruins of postwar Eastern Europe. "Ukrainian people. Many thousands of Ukrainians are in displaced persons camps in Germany. Their eyes are turned to you. Ukrainians! Help them come to free American land. IT IS OUR SACRED DUTY," trumpeted one flier about a community-wide effort to complete immigration applications for as many Ukrainians as possible. "Hurry, because we precede other nations and they are exhausting the immigration quotas. Come and complete applications — for those that have family, for your family. For those that have friends — for your friends. For those who don't have family or friends, come and help those for whom we have a name and address."

By 1945, like a number of Ukrainians, John and Mike Mazur had left the Southside for Parma, a suburb of modest single-family homes just beyond Cleveland's southwest boundary. Their churches, including St. Vladimir's, steadily followed suit. Mike again started to prepare to bring his family to the United States. Yet the effort proceeded at an agonizingly slow pace. The hurricane of the war had deposited millions of Ukrainians in displaced persons camps in Germany, where the chaos that prevailed gave the authorities a vested interested in resettling people.

Mike's family wasn't there, though — in 1945, before they were arrested and sent to Siberia, the Mazurs had become trapped inside the Soviet Union, five miles east of the border between Poland and Ukrainian Soviet Socialist Republic. It could take up to six months for a letter to reach Staryava from Cleveland. In the midst of this agonizing period, Mike's brother, John, was diagnosed with cancer. The disease ate away at his lungs and throat. In July 1946, he died, only fifty years old.

Mike would remain close to John's wife Helen and John Jr., his nephew, but with his brother's death he lost the only family

member who had come from the same place he had, who could recall Staryava in his heart and mind. Before the Mazurs could make
any headway on the move, politics again intervened, and Mike's
family was in Siberia.

There's nothing left of that time, no one who can tell me what
Mike experienced when he realized his family was no longer in
Staryava. Yet it does not require much creativity to imagine the
guilt and despair he must have felt. To think that he had been in
Cleveland, working at the bakery, safe and sound, while his family
was destroyed!

Somehow, some way, word of his family's fate got to Mike.
My grandmother told me that the Red Cross had helped her father
locate them in Siberia, and indeed the Red Cross did provide these
kinds of reunification services, utilizing the International Tracing
Service and other resources. By 1955, eight years after they were
exiled, documents show that Mike had located his family in Yemanzhelinsk.

By then, even his own life looked somewhat different. In 1948,
two years after John died, Helen had married an affable Polish man
named John Lacki. Leaving the newlyweds on their own, Mike returned to the Southside, this time taking an apartment further
down West Fourteenth Street, closer to St. Vladimir's. He had a big
Buick that he would drive across the city to his job at Hough Bakery, a confectionary revered throughout Cleveland for its cakes,
strudels, and sweet buns. In December 1955, with the help of John
Bilinski, a local powerbroker of Ukrainian descent, he filed an affidavit in support of Rozalia's application for a visa. "Affiant says
that since he and his wife, Rozalia Mazur, are nearing 60 years of
age, that they are in the last part of their lives and for their remaining years of their lives he would wish to have his wife spend with
him," the document reads. "Affiant further says that he has a strong
sense of moral responsibility for his wife."

Within three months, the U.S. Embassy in Moscow approved
Rozalia's request for a visa. To celebrate, Mike went house-hunting.
Almost thirty years after he had come to America, he was again
trying to make good on the dream that had brought him here:

providing a proper home for his family. In November, he used virtually all his savings to buy two lots on West Forty-Sixth Street,
paying the cost in full. Two three-story houses sat on the property,
and a small cottage was tucked away in the back, near an alley that
ran parallel to the street. The area, known as Clark-Fulton, was
even rougher than the neighboring Southside. But safety had never
been much of a concern for Mike, who dealt with crime as he did
the other complexities of American life: by barreling through it.

Mike had purposedly sought out a property with three structures. His wife was just the start. He would bring his two surviving
children, too. Anna had three daughters now—the youngest, my
mother, Nadia, was just two years old. And Ivan already had a son,
Ihor, who was a few years older. The houses on West Forty-Sixth
Street were just across the street from a public elementary school.

But the months passed, and there was no reply from the Soviet
authorities about Rozalia's exit visa. In October 1956, Mike again
called upon the services of Bilinski. Together they wrote and sent
letters to the highest authorities in the Soviet Union, Nikita Khrush-
chev and Nikolai Bulganin, about the matter. Each was on the let-
terhead of the Cleveland City Council, on which Bilinski served.
"Up to the present time, such permission [for an exit visa] has not
been granted, and I sincerely beg you to look into this matter at
your convenience to see if it is possible for my wife to join me in
America in the remaining years of our lives," Mike wrote.

The Soviet Ministry of Internal Affairs received the letter a
week later. Within two weeks, it had them both translated into Russian. But the authorities were not so prompt in following up with
Mike. In 1957, the Soviet regime dismissed Mike's request after re-
viewing the files on Rozalia's exile and Stefan's UPA involvement.

Back in Clark-Fulton, the only thing Mike could do was wait.
Hope and wait. He lived in the smallest of the three houses on his
property and lodged boarders in the two larger houses. He did as
he, and other Ukrainian Americans, had always done—he sent his
family packages filled with American sundries. Throughout their
childhood, my mom and Olga had matching jackets to fight the Siberian winter and boots that could find traction on the mud of the

unpaved streets. They had sweaters in cheery colors that they wore around New Year's. What the family couldn't use, they sold. They had more than a lot of other people in their circumstances, but their prosperity was relative. As a young girl, my mother once told me, she yearned for colored pencils. She had not seen such a fine thing herself in Siberia and the stores were depressing and empty, but she had gotten the idea that they existed, and she impressed upon her mother how much she wanted them. And my grandmother — likely through a window that her father Mike had opened for them with his valuable American packages — was somehow able to get them for her young daughters.

On January 7, 1960, there came a break: The Presidium of the Supreme Soviet issued a decree terminating the exile of Rozalia, Anna, and Ivan Mazur. It was followed a week later by an order from the Ministry of Internal Affairs requiring the dismantling of the special settlements. By March 1960, more than twelve years after they were exiled, Rozalia, Anna, and Ivan received official word that they were free to leave Chelyabinsk Oblast. The freedom came with stipulations. They could not move back to the oblast they had come from, and the property the Soviet authorities had seized from them in Ukraine would not be returned, nor would any compensation be offered.

It was, I'm sure, a moment of joy, but also of frustration, even anger. Being free to leave did not equate with having somewhere to go. In the Soviet system, even citizens without strikes against them were fenced in through the regime's *propiska* registration system, which required citizens to receive permission from the state to move to a new location. The scheme was set up to mitigate the deluge of migrants into cities after the war, and persisted for decades — and still exists in some form in Russia — as a rudimentary tool for population control.

For Soviet citizens recently released from exile, the barriers were even more confounding. To get a registration pass in a certain locale, you had to have a job in that place. But to get a job, you had to have a registration pass. The places where this contradiction was alleviated were where the regime needed workers — and often these

locations had a bleakness on the order of the Siberian exile settlements, even those in Ukraine. But for the millions of people who
had been displaced through Soviet exile and were now permitted
to return to their countries of origin, it was an easy choice. There
was no question about it—they wanted to be among their people,
to be in their homeland, even if it wasn't their former home exactly.
Overwhelmingly, they returned.

Ivan and his family left Yemanzhelinsk first. Ivan's prospects
of getting an exit visa to immigrate to the United States were close
to nil. First of all, the Soviet regime was reluctant to allow able-bodied men to emigrate, given the great numbers that had been lost
during the war. Second, Ivan wasn't just the brother of an UPA
fighter. He was a former gulag labor camp prisoner who had once
been found guilty of treason against the Soviet Union. Though he
had been relieved of the harshest terms of his sentence, he was still
a first-order "enemy of the people" in the eyes of the state. These
people were not the kind who got scarce exit visas.

Ivan and his wife found jobs in Chervonohrad, a coal-mining
town in western Ukraine. The snow that fell heavily on the city in
the winter often grew black when it accumulated on the ground.
They moved there with their three children in 1965.

For my grandmother, the decisions were more complicated.
By 1962, the tumultuous marriage between my grandparents had
reached its violent nadir, and my grandmother had initiated divorce proceedings. A de facto pariah amid the Ukrainians of Yemanzhelinsk, Andriy returned to western Ukraine. Now a single
man, he managed to evade the *propiska* regulators. Within months
of the divorce becoming final, Andriy got a Khyriv war widow
pregnant. With her help, he was able to secure the papers that
would allow him to stay in Khyriv without hindrance. They had
Luba—her full name, "Lyubov," means love in Ukrainian—and
married.

My grandmother, still in Yemanzhelinsk, was now the sole
provider for three daughters. The end of her marriage came with a
number of silver livings, one of which was that her bid to emigrate
was more likely to be successful because she had no husband, no

man to deny the Soviet state. But emigration was far from a fore-gone conclusion, given how infrequently exit visas were granted. She needed a realistic plan.

Because of the harshness and difficulty of their work, the state allowed coal miners to retire at age forty-five. My grandmother would be forty-five in 1970. She resolved to stay in Siberia until then, so that when she moved back to Ukraine she could do so with a pension and without the need to find another job. Ivan was just three years younger than her but did not have the tenure that she did, due to his time in the gulag labor camp. Many people in similar circumstances made equivalent calculations. The result was that, even though the exiles detested the terms, many stayed on for years after their sentences were canceled.

In the summer of 1961, suddenly, unexpectedly, life-changing news arrived in Yemanzhelinsk: Rozalia Mazur, my great-grandmother, had been granted an exit visa to leave the Soviet Union and immi-grate to the United States to join her husband, Mike. His hard work had paid off: Rozalia would be one of the few Soviet citizens to re-ceive the privilege. A heart-pounding scramble ensued—the win-dow of validity for exit visas was notoriously short and the visa petition Mike had acquired for his wife from the American author-ities in 1956 had expired and needed to be revalidated. Working with John Bilinski, the local powerbroker, Mike updated and refiled his affidavit and the evidence that he could support his wife. The lawyers labored to impress upon the relevant agencies how urgent the situation was. "PLEASE EXPEDITE" blared a note the U.S. Em-bassy in Moscow sent to the Cleveland office of the Immigration and Naturalization Services about Rozalia's visa revalidation in August of that year. "A Soviet exit visa has been issued to the peti-tion beneficiary and only a limited time remains before its expira-tion. Renewal of such visas is a difficult, time-consuming, and fre-quently unsuccessful process."

This time, fortune favored my great-grandparents. In early September, U.S. authorities revalidated Rozalia's visa petition. By October 11, Rozalia had traveled the three thousand miles from

Yemanzhelinsk to Moscow to complete the medical exams and in-terviews at the U.S. Embassy necessary for immigration. The sun-dries that Mike had been sending for years paid off, literally—the family could ably absorb the cost of the huge transition. Rozalia said goodbye to her children and grandchildren—by then, life must have taught her she stood a good chance of not seeing them again. A week later, on October 18, Rozalia was on a Scandinavian Air-lines flight from Moscow en route to Cleveland.

What occupied Rozalia in the long hours she flew over Europe and the Atlantic Ocean? She hadn't seen her husband in thirty-two years. When they had last laid eyes on each other, she was a comely young mother—a woman you could believe would have attracted suitors in her husband's absence, a woman whose sociability and health were apparent enough that you would think she might have wanted to entertain them. But by the time the war was over and the family was in Siberia, she had become virtually unrecognizable. Her striking features had been stretched and muddled by age; her lips had shriveled. She had about her an air of frailty, perhaps the result of a bout of scarlet fever during which she had lost her hair. It had grown back, though. Now it was darker, with a tinge of red, and it was infamous in the family because it would never lose its color. Not that you would have seen this hair much—like all mar-ried Soviet women, she wore a babushka, or kerchief, tightly around her head. What would she have cared about her looks? Her eldest son was dead. Her brother was dead. Her suitor, Punko, if that's what he had been, was dead. And her husband was all but unknown to her.

Now she was sixty-one, and she was entering a world that was not filled with death, though ghosts were everywhere, but was in-stead filled with life. Life and hope. A world where people smiled all the time—for photos, in greeting to others when they walked down the street—people they might not even *know*. Not that she would guessed that before she left—all she would have known was what Mike would have been able to get past the censors—maybe something like, *I'll take care of you. We'll have everything we need.* Could he have written about the car, the house, his tenure at the bakery? Could Rozalia have even believed such possibilities, reading his letters in hardscrabble Yemanzhelinsk? Soviet propaganda laid the lies on thick about the decrepitude and poverty of the United States. Who would you believe—your longlost spouse or your lying state?

Perhaps the bond between my great-grandparents was strong enough that thirty-two years, a war, and possible other lovers couldn't vanquish it. Perhaps Rozalia knew in her heart that Mike wouldn't leave her, that he would be on her side for good. But she must have felt the choice to come to America to be a risk. I think that she felt that risk and went anyway. Rozalia was stubborn, but tweak her situation a bit and you can see that, even more, she was *brave*. She did what she wanted. She relied on herself. She added to the belongings she brought with her on her flight from Moscow an apple. If there was nothing to eat in this new country, as everyone said, at least she would have that.

Five years passed between the immigration of my great-grandmother Rozalia and that of my grandmother, my mother, and my aunt Olga. In 1966, when their applications were approved, my mom was twelve, Olga fourteen. By then my grandmother had secured a proper one-story house in Yemanzhelinsk that had wooden walls and shutters and an outhouse in the backyard. The girls shared a bed. Like everyone, they had a dog, a dark German shepherd mix named Tarzan. Every Saturday, they went to the *banya* to wash. In the winter, they wore *valenki*, felt boots whose shafts covered their knees, to ward off the high drifts of snow that could accumulate as early as September and didn't start to melt until March. Once a year, the family got a piglet. The girls fed him and doted on him until the fall, when one of the adults slaughtered him and the family turned him into sausages.

Stefa had not applied to leave. By that time, she was married and the mother of a young boy, Volodya—two sure obstacles to success with the Soviet emigration system. The choice for her to stay behind was wrenching; the family was effectively divided in two. Ivan's inability to leave Ukraine and join his family in the

United States, in particular, was a longstanding source of pain to his father. Mike had bought the multi-structure property on West Forty-Sixth Street purposely — to have enough room for the families of both of his children. The house he purchased for Ivan would never be filled with its intended occupants. Every day it would be an outsized reminder of Ivan's absence, the split that the war had dealt that would never heal.

Mike would spend the last years of his life contemplating ways to finagle his son's exit from the Soviet Union. In 1970, he made a trip to Soviet Ukraine to see Ivan and Stefa, who had returned to Ukraine after her mother and sisters left for the United States. The last time Mike had seen his son, Ivan had been on the verge of toddlerhood, just learning to walk. Now he was middle-aged and a father of three. It would be their only meeting. Later in the 1970s, Mike suffered a severe stroke. He spent the rest of his life in a nursing home in suburban Cleveland, where he was visited regularly by the doting Rozalia until her death in 1982.

Because of the widespread suspicion of the United States, my grandmother instructed Nadia and Olga to tell their friends that they were immigrating to Canada. When the time came for the family to leave Yemanzhelinsk for good, Nadia cried and clung to Stefa. It would take twenty-five years and the dawn of a different world order for them to see each other again.

Anna and the girls first traveled to Moscow, where they had medical tests and final interviews with the U.S. Embassy. They acted like tourists for the first time in their lives, taking a cruise down the Moscow River and purchasing postcards of the Kremlin and other landmarks. My grandmother spent down her last rubles at GUM, Moscow's premier department store on Red Square, buying a set of gold-plated spoons with filigrees along the stems. While their value is not great, today we keep those spoons in a safe.

Their flight out of the Soviet Union came at the end of December 1966. The flight attendants were charmed by the quiet, polite girls who didn't know any English and doted on them the whole flight. In the sky over Europe, Olga and Nadia tried soda for the first time.

Their entry into the U.S. was not as pleasant. Their flight from Moscow landed at John F. Kennedy Airport in New York City, but their connecting flight to Cleveland left from LaGuardia. They deplaned into a bustling JFK without knowing how to get to their next stop. My grandmother had befriended a Lithuanian woman on the flight who was in the same position. The four of them huddled in a corner of the terminal, growing more bewildered and despondent with each confident, indifferent American who passed by. My mother started to cry. The Lithuanian woman started to cry. Stifling panic, my grandmother spied a sign across the room. "INFORMATION," it read. Its meaning clicked — *informacja* was a word my grandmother knew from her Polish schooling so many years ago. She steered the group to the desk and with the help of an attendant who spoke Polish figured out how to make their way to LaGuardia.

Mykhailo and Rozalia — or Mike and Rose as they were known in the United States — greeted the weary travelers at the airport gate in Cleveland the evening of December 30. The adults dabbed tissues at their eyes to mop up their tears. My mother carried her most treasured possessions in bags that hung heavily from her fists: hardcover volumes of Russian literature and grammar and a red velvet scrapbook of black-and-white headshots of Soviet movie stars she had assembled herself. As they rode from the airport to the Mazur home on West Forty-Sixth Street, Olga and Nadia marveled at the city's display of Christmas lights. They had never seen anything so beautiful.

For the second time in her life, my grandmother was starting over in a foreign land, where she knew neither the language nor the customs nor the system of governance. But as much as it was new, it was also a return.

That night, for the first time since she was four years old, my grandmother slept under the same roof as both of her parents.

Starting over would not be easy for my grandmother, but as with all challenges, the burden was relative. No longer did work mean long hours in the cold, damp confines of the mines, but sitting at a table in a brightly lit factory among other women her age, sorting and stacking clean motor parts. No longer did learning a new language entail studying castoff remnants of newsprint, but taking free classes at a nearby public library. No longer did being a daughter amount to some mixture of fear and longing, but being a companion and witness during her parents' last years and inevitable declines. No longer did sacrifice mean standing in a queue at a store that might not even have food to sell, but walking the two miles to work instead of taking the city bus, so that she could save the fare for her daughters' future college tuitions.

The challenges would ease soon enough. Her parents needed new silverware because Mike had obtained all of his from promotional giveaways at the gas station. My grandmother would find herself red-faced in the grocery store after asking a befuddled stock clerk for *monkey*, a word she confused with a garbled version of the Polish word for flour. The property on West Forty-Sixth Street had enough space for a large garden, and the soil was rich enough and the growing season long enough that she could plant tomatoes, squash, and cucumbers.

Her girls made good on her greatest aspiration, which was for them to finish college. They had enrolled in Cleveland's public schools without knowing a word of English, but with remediation and, just as important, American television, they soon spoke Ukrainian only with their mother and between themselves, on the playground, when they wanted to keep their exchanges secret. But their success didn't come in the exact form my grandmother wanted. Olga insisted on moving to Columbus to get her degree at Ohio State University, and Nadia spent only a year at home as a Cleveland State student before she rented an apartment on the city's west side. My grandmother was confused and somewhat insulted by her daughters' attempts to stake out lives of their own, perhaps because it was only late in life that she had been granted that freedom.

Slowly, my grandmother created a life whose fullness had its own power. She worked. She had hobbies and passions and people who cared about her. The distance she had traveled between her origins and the life she made in the United States would occasionally strike her and she would find herself thinking of her past quizzically, as if it were a stranger's story and not her own. "Sometimes I think, was it me there or not?" she said.

Of course, she could not entirely leave her experience behind. She said off-color things occasionally. She railed too strongly against her daughters for embracing the comforts of American life. She exercised a manic vigilance about food and money. But the worst parts of what she had suffered, and what she might have thought or believed, lessened in the bloom of her later years. She was, by the end of her life, transformed by her own efforts and the best promise of this country, which is to say that she became who she wanted to be, not what the world had conspired to make her.

Epilogue

In the summer of 2021, I decided to try training in psychoanalysis, a pursuit that necessitated moving to New York City, where I had lived for a few years in my twenties. I rented an apartment a few blocks from the Brooklyn waterfront. Sometimes when I strolled along it, I imagined Mike sailing up the East River in 1929 aboard the SS *Leviathan*, smoke billowing from its row of stacks.

For a while, the vision was just a curiosity, an uncanny resonance of my life with his. Then these resonances began to multiply in ways I had never imagined. I put aside my psychoanalytic studies. I had lost interest in thinking about how family history reverberates in the psyche over many years. Elements of my family's experience were repeating themselves in the world — now.

Russia's invasion of Ukraine at the beginning of 2022 gave me a much better sense of the distress Mike felt as he watched from afar as war consumed his family and homeland. I now felt a degree of it myself. I felt shaky when I checked the news each morning. Images of bombed apartment buildings and destroyed bridges floated through my mind when I tried to fall asleep. When cars backfired, my heart raced, momentarily convinced that bombs were falling in Brooklyn. I felt helpless as I tried to brainstorm ways to alleviate the pain of my loved ones.

Of course, there were many differences in our experiences — among them the fact that it was much easier to maintain contact than it had been in Mike's day. I could easily message my Ukrainian relatives on WhatsApp and Facebook. And distance was not what it had been. Two months after the war began, I flew to Italy to see my cousin Natalia, who had left Ukraine with her two adolescent daughters, Anya and Olha, when the war started.

On many counts, Natalia and the girls were lucky. They went to Italy because they had a family connection — years earlier, the mother of Natalia's husband, Vasyl, had moved to the country and married an Italian man. As soon as the war broke out, Natalia's in-laws urged her to bring the girls from Truskavets and come live with them in a town outside Bologna.

I rolled into town on a bright spring morning aboard one of Italy's sleek regional trains. Natalia and Anya were at the station to greet me. There was no greater marker of the passage of time than Anya, who at fourteen was a foot taller than when I last saw her a few years earlier.

The town they were staying in was full of typical Italian charm—piazzas, *gelaterias*, lush flowers tumbling from hanging baskets—but as we walked from the train station, it was Ukraine that loomed. I knew the gist of Natalia and the girls' departure from Ukraine but hadn't bothered them for details. (Refugees are busy people). As we settled into their apartment on a leafy central street, Natalia told me the full story.

Like most Ukrainians, Natalia and Vasyl had considered a Russian invasion unthinkable. When it happened, Vasyl, who had been working a trucking gig in the EU, abandoned his job and rushed back to his family. He urged Natalia to leave Ukraine with the girls. (By that point, martial law had been imposed, and as a man under sixty, he was barred from leaving the country.)

Natalia was deeply conflicted. She was a patriot and had no desire to abandon her homeland in its hour of need. She also was loath to be separated from Vasyl and their son, Roman, who, because he was over eighteen, was also required to remain in Ukraine. Natalia's mother, my aunt Stefa, had turned eighty the previous summer and, like many older people, categorically refused to leave. But Natalia knew that the environment was unpredictable and, even in western Ukraine, possibly dangerous. It wasn't a good place for kids.

The first weekend after the invasion, Natalia agreed to check out the situation at the train station in Lviv, the travel hub closest to their home in Truskavets. By then, it had been widely reported that the station was overrun with would-be refugees. Natalia suspected that they wouldn't be able to board a train and would just come back to Truskavets. Still, she and the girls packed small backpacks with food and their documents. Knowing that people had been standing in closely-packed quarters for hours to board trains, they wore diapers.

When Natalia, Vasyl, and the girls arrived at the station in Lviv, it was teeming with people trying to flee. They luckily got in through a side entrance that allowed them to bypass the bulk of the crowd, and quickly found themselves beside the railway tracks. They ran toward a group of men in military fatigues who were knocking on a door of a train about to depart. Turned away, the men dispersed. The family remained on the platform, uncertain what to do next. Then the door opened and Natalia and the girls were pulled aboard. Within moments of them stepping onto the train, the door closed behind them and the wheels started to churn. They had made it. They had barely had a chance to say goodbye to Vasyl.

The train was moving, but going where? This was the question Natalia focused on as she sought to steady herself. None of the people around them had an idea. All anyone knew was that the train was going west. Eventually, Natalia found a conductor. "Where are we going?" she asked him.

"To Poland," the conductor answered unhelpfully. He didn't seem to know any more than the others.

In comparison to many other Ukrainian refugees that weekend, Natalia and the girls traveled in relative comfort—there were only six people in their coupe car, which normally sat four. Once they crossed the border into Poland, volunteers came aboard the train and offered them medication, food, water, and tea.

About twenty hours after they left Lviv, they got off the train somewhere in rural southeastern Poland. Natalia deflected offers for help and hurried the girls into a waiting taxi. She asked the driver to take them to the nearest airport.

That turned out to be Katowice's. On her phone, Natalia found a flight from Katowice to Bologna that was leaving in a few hours. But when she tried to buy the tickets, the transaction wouldn't go through, perhaps because of cyberattacks on Ukrainian banks— there were rumors of such disruptions that day. When she told me this part of the story, I thought of our grandmother's moment of panic when she had to make sense of New York's multiple airports after arriving with my mom and Olga from the Soviet Union. Fifty-six years later, her granddaughter was also momentarily stymied while at an airport in a foreign country with her two youngest children, trying to outrun Moscow's reach.

As Natalia considered what to do, her phone rang. The caller was a friend, a Ukrainian who happened to live in Warsaw. Natalia told him what was going on. The friend offered to buy them the tickets. She sent the friend photos of their documents, and the transaction went through. By eight p.m., twenty-eight hours after Natalia and the girls left Truskavets, they had arrived at Vasyl's mother's home outside Bologna and started a chapter of their lives whose ending was a question mark.

In peaceful Italy, Natalia and the girls were in the habit of counting their blessings. Unlike so many Ukrainian refugees, they had a place where they could stay indefinitely, in an area that was familiar to them. They had the means to cover their modest expenses. The girls had plenty of experience with distance education due to the COVID pandemic, and after a two-week war-induced break, they resumed online lessons with their school in Truskavets. They even had their most-needed belongings. Buses had started transporting refugees' luggage from Ukraine to Italy, and Vasyl had sent them suitcases packed with clothes and other longed-for items they hadn't been able to bring with them when they left.

It was a delight to be with Natalia and the girls, and I was grateful that after so much time apart we could enjoy each day's languid flow together. We went to different grocery stores to pick out provisions for dinner. Anya beat me several times at chess. Olha gathered seedlings for a garden she hoped to tend that summer. In the evenings, we watched films in Ukrainian that Anya found online.

But sadness hung in the air. One day, Natalia walked me through some recent photos on her phone: They showed Roman on his motorcycle, the girls doing yoga stretches on a beach near Odesa, family gathered in Truskavets for Olha's twelfth birthday party in December. Natalia played a video of Olha unwrapping her main present, a guitar, her face a picture of delight. I could hear the voices of my loved ones in the background. Melancholy washed over me. Because of COVID, it had been so long since I had seen them. Though I knew we would meet again, it seemed impossible that our future gatherings would ever be so carefree. "It's nice that the phone reminds you of these moments," Natalia said, interrupting my thoughts. A moment later, she added, "But also hard."

Before I went to Italy, I had gone back to Cleveland and picked up a watch of my grandmother's that my mother had held on to. It was a simple but pretty, plated in rose-gold. My grandmother had purchased it in the Soviet Union, possibly at GUM when she was trying to spend down her spare rubles before she flew with my mom and aunt Olga to the United States. She had worn it all the time, and I thought Natalia might like to have it.

I gave it to her one afternoon after we had finished lunch.

"Is this our grandmother's?" Natalia asked as soon as she pulled it of the small jewelry bag I had kept it in. I nodded. She immediately started to cry.

I went over and put my arms around her. "It's so you can have a part of her with you now," I said. "Some of her strength."

"I don't know how she did it," she said, the words stumbling out. I rubbed her back and looked across the kitchen table at Anya and Olha, whose faces had grown somber. For a moment, I imagined us being joined by my grandmother in this little Italian kitchen. What would she say to us, I wondered? What wisdom would she impart from the years of hardship, destruction, and violence she had endured?

The answer came to me immediately. It was simple: *Live.*

Afterword

I researched and drafted most of this book in the second half of the 2010s, at the comfortable remove of more than 70 years from its most difficult episodes, naively confident that such struggles would never be repeated on wide swaths of Ukrainian soil. By that point, Russia's annexation of Crimea and occupation of eastern Ukraine had metamorphosized into a "frozen conflict" that, while grim, seemed destined to stay that way. If anything, the history I was looking back at fascinated me because it seemed so distant and improbable.

Now all of that has changed. Bombs leveling Ukrainian cities, terrified civilians hiding in shelters for months, families torn apart, Ukrainians deported to Siberia, the steppe pockmarked with mass graves — these horrors have moved inexorably from history books and archives to the Ukrainian present. While I have experienced virtually all of them at a remove, moderated by a screen, they have a proximity unlike any I had known before.

Russia's full-scale invasion of Ukraine in 2022 made me think somewhat differently about my family's story. As my social media feeds filled with obituaries of Ukrainians who had died fighting the Russian army, I realized how academic my focus had been, how much I had been trying to pinpoint the side of history on which my family had landed. I had undertaken this work largely ignorant of the feelings that I would now sum up with the words *fear spurred by existential threat*. I understood this concept before the invasion, of course. I would have even considered myself capable of describing the feeling. It was another thing entirely, however, to live within that feeling, even just a little bit.

As the Russian army bombed, tortured, raped, and murdered its way through Ukraine for most of 2022, I came to appreciate for the first time in my life how defending your country could be more important than a political agenda — more important, even, than your own survival. I understood this because I saw clearly that for Ukrainians today, to live under Russia — to have their vocations curtailed, their speech restricted, their movement policed, their

language suppressed, their possessions and property destroyed —
would be to die a different kind of death.

Was this the calculus animating Stefan when he signed up for
the Ukrainian auxiliary police or the OUN-SB — that he and his family had no hope for a life worth living under an alternative regime?
I don't mean to dismiss or excuse the disturbing, repugnant things
Stefan likely believed and did as part of these institutions when I
write this. I merely want to express that I sense how his choice to
serve in them may have been more equivocal than I thought, that
his choice came amid a terrifying feeling whose edges I am newly
able to grasp.

Or maybe not. Before the war, I had thought this book would
lead me to better understand my forebears. To some extent it has.
And yet, as I tracked how much my own sense of their experience
was changed even by my limited exposure to the current war, my
belief that this deeper understanding was possible was tempered. I
had been protected greatly by my year of birth and citizenship, I
realized; these things would always buffer me from the reality of
my forebears' experience. I have never quite obtained the feeling of
rest Virginia Woolf said she experienced when she finished *To the
Lighthouse*, her tribute to her mother, who died when Woolf was
thirteen. Even when I thought I had answered all the questions I
could possibly ask about my family's past, life would shift, and new
questions would emerge.

I chose the phrase "Ukraine is not dead yet" — from the first line of
the country's national anthem — as the title of this book prior to the
Russian invasion. I liked how aptly it dramatized Ukraine's long,
arduous struggle for independence. Yet it resonated with me as
more than just a commentary on the country's political status. It
reminded me of how Ukraine lived on in my grandmother's
memory, often as a site of trauma, long after she immigrated to the
United States, and how that legacy worked on me by making me a
person who tried to save that history from being forgotten.

It is difficult to sum up what I learned by researching my
grandmother's life in such depth. I didn't start this endeavor

naively. From early adulthood, I understood that my family had been adherents of Ukrainian nationalism, and that the movement had the uncomfortable history of being allied with Nazi Germany. I was well aware that people had their reasons for staying quiet about their pasts, especially in the former Soviet Union, where many had been schooled in the consequences of revealing too much to the wrong person.

Perhaps I can only say that once I started researching my grandmother's life, it became impossible not to finish. The reasons for this, as a psychoanalyst would say, are "overdetermined" — consisting of multiple factors that may overlap and contradict themselves. I knew if I did not commit my grandmother's life to paper an immense range of experience would disappear. Living in her story was a way to give her a degree of companionship that for long stretches of her life eluded her. Part of me was, I think, trying to correct the assumption I had made as a child: that her life, long, foreign, and out of step with American popular culture, was not worth looking at too deeply. At the same time, writing this book was an act of rebellion, a way to work against the silences my grandmother and mother had placed on our family story. Penetrating those silences was a form of individuation, a way to turn the history I was born into something I didn't so much passively receive as actively make.

I cared, too, because my grandmother's story was complicated. If her life had been simple, if there had always been a clear lesson, I would have found it less interesting, and whatever I could wring from it much less persuasive. It was precisely the story's murkiness that made me feel that it contained something worth knowing. As a person drawn to difficult moral questions, I got satisfaction from turning the story over and over again in my mind to figure out what I could learn.

My attraction to the complex is also partly why I fell in love with Ukraine. Through my travels and relationships, I have seen a country that is home to so much joy and so much sorrow, so much striving and so much dysfunction, so much to be proud of and so much to atone for. It saddens me deeply that the protest expressed in the line "Ukraine is not dead yet" feels relevant again. I had no idea when I was writing this book that I was also documenting the Ukraine I had come to know and love, as that country in many respects is gone.

What the new Ukraine will be is a hard question to pose. The possible answers are harder still. To me, two things are clear.

The first is that the task of building a new Ukraine will be complicated—full of moments of light and darkness and replete with concerns that cannot be easily resolved.

The second is that Ukraine has a new pantheon of heroes to draw on, men and women who have sacrificed everything for their beautiful, imperfect, singular country.

Acknowledgments

This book was a family effort in more ways than one. My aunt Stefa Schutyak has proved not just my namesake but my guardian angel—I could never properly thank her for tolerating all those trips to the *selo* and all my questions about the past. My cousin Natalia Humetska has an intuition and grace that has been a balm to me for decades, and was fundamental to making a country that seemed so different at first come to feel like home.

I'm grateful to Anastasia Yurystovska, the late Andriy Bandriwsky, Slavik Mazur, Olha Zhuk, and Stefa Ostafinska for sharing the lives they lived under the shadow of war and its aftermath. My grandmother's brother, the late Ivan Mazur, guided me around Staryava several times and told me about his childhood there. My aunt Luba Kokhan helped me understand our family's experience in rural western Ukraine and took me across the border for an important trip to my grandfather's native village of Liskowate, now in Poland. Maria Zhuk was always ready with a warm smile and helping hand in Staryava. Mary Mazur dusted off decades-old memories about the Cleveland lives of Mike and Rose Mazur.

Lida Borokha went above and beyond as a cousin, friend, and occasional co-researcher. Ihor and the late Tanya Mazur put me up in Kyiv time and time again and advised on family history and life in the capital. Anya and Olha Humetska delight me and make me confident in Ukraine's bright future. I would have been nowhere (literally) without Vasyl Humetsky's calm, easygoing manner and driving skills. I also thank Ira Borokha, Volodya Schutyak, Roman Humetsky, Andriy Kokhan, Slavik Schutyak, and the rest of my Ukrainian family for their many years of love and openness.

A number of scholars and experts informed the research that went into this book. Marta Mudri at the Ukrainian Museum-Archives in Cleveland conducted a sensitive and probing interview with my grandmother in 2009 under the auspices of its oral history project. At the U.S. Holocaust Memorial Museum, Vincent Slatt provided priceless assistance, context, and encouragement. David

Rich kindly offered his counsel about the Ukrainian auxiliary police and provided essential historical feedback. So much of what I know about Ukraine rests on the foundation of the stories and insights of Olesia Shchur, who, years ago in Orange Revolution-era Lviv, spent hours and hours telling me about her experience growing up in Soviet and post-Soviet Ukraine.

Jared McBride answered my endless questions and gave me a model for how to treat the most difficult chapters of Ukrainian history comprehensively and judiciously. He also provided extensive, probing comments on this manuscript for which I am most thankful. John-Paul Himka and Omer Bartov also provided helpful comments. Marta Havryshko, Oksana Kis, Andriy Usach, Olha Honchar, Leonid Heretz, Yevheniia Moliar, Sofia Dyak, Georgiy Kasianov, Vyacheslav Likhachev, Pavel Tikhonovski, Dmytro Soloviov, Oleksandr Pahiria, Sasha Nazar, and others met with me at various points to share their expertise and experience, and it helped me think about this story more deeply. Needless to say, all choices (and mistakes) are my own.

Victor Kuzio, Alex Dunai, Serhiy Myzychuk, and Maciej Orzechowski helped me obtain family records from archives in Poland and Ukraine—a task that, as this book chronicles, requires a resourcefulness of the highest order. Olga and Maxime Lachasse, Yuliya Riabukha, and Elena Volkava provided transcription and translation assistance over the years.

Zoryana Martsinkovska and Klaus Hasbron-Blume helped me meet Stefania Midyanka in Staryava, and Andriy Usach, Anna Yatsenko, and their research team conducted the interview with her and added it to their remarkable trove of Ukrainian oral histories at the Territory of Terror Museum. I'm grateful that Staryava has such a careful custodian of its past as Stefania, and that she was open to sharing her memories with us. Shoshana Oref graciously shared her family's memories of Jewish Staryava.

This book got its start as my thesis at the Goucher College non-fiction MFA program, the first of several institutions that helped it come into being. I'm indebted to Suzannah Lessard, Jacob Levenson, Diana Hume George, and Wil Hylton for their mentorship and to my fellow students and alums for their encouragement and guidance amid the daunting process of book publishing, especially Porscha Burke, Stephanie Gorton, Kristina Gaddy, Neda Toloui-Semnani, and Theo Emery. I'm particularly glad that Brooke MacMillan and Katie Gilbert have become close colleagues and friends.

After graduating, I had the good fortune to receive a Logan Nonfiction Fellowship at the Carey Institute for Global Good to continue to develop this book. I was just as lucky to be there at the same time as a number of inspiring journalists whom I now count as friends, among them Jonathan Meiburg, Elena Horn, Alessandro Leonardi, Finbarr O'Reilly, and Jude Joffe-Block. I'm grateful to Carly Willsie, Josh Friedman, Jonathan Logan, and the rest of the Logan team for keeping this gift of an institution going. While I was in London, the London Library Emerging Fellows Program provided the workspace of my dreams.

When it came time to bring this book out into the world, I was aided by a number of talented people. Andreas Umland brought it into the fold of his excellent Ukrainian Voices series at ibidem Press while Katharina Bedorf and and Jana Dävers provided the administrative acumen that made its publication happen. Pete Beatty and Katie Hall edited versions of the manuscript. Vincent Ercolano, copy editor extraordinaire, also took his pen to it. Tom Howey designed the cover and Tetyana Melnyk the family tree. Rob McQuilken and Max Moorhead offered feedback and counsel on publishing matters, and Megan Posco provided excellent publicity support.

Many supported me in a personal way. More than 10 years ago in Berlin, I was lucky to cross paths with Sonia Smith, a fellow *Kyiv Post* alum. Our ensuing friendship has been a great joy to me, and her sharp mind, journalistic acumen, and expertise in the former Soviet space have made her an essential interlocutor during the long haul of this project. Sonia (and Margot in utero) accompanied me on an important trip to Ukraine in 2018.

For various forms of help along the way, I thank Gustavo Guerra, Winny Chen, Jitinder Kohli, Darcy Courteau, Randy Rosenthal, Gabriel Heller, and my extended circle of wonderful friends. I'm particularly indebted to Kathy Atlass, whose wisdom has been long been a guiding light for me. This book would likely not exist without her, as she literally suggested it.

My parents, Allen and Nadia, my brothers, Alex and Mike, and aunt Olga Barth lived much of this story alongside me, and their encouragement and interest kept me going. My mother and Olga read and critiqued the manuscript and scoured their memories for details that would make it richer. I also thank my cousins Emerson and Miles Barth for their companionship at St. Vlad's luncheons and everything that has come since.

My love for my grandmother Anna is what animated this book. Ukrainians commonly wish the dead *vichnaya pamyat* – eternal memory. That memory is meant to be within the eyes of God, but I think the human kind is just as valuable. This book is my attempt to give that to her.

Sources

Twentieth century Ukrainian history has a strong scholarly and cre-
ative tradition that is only growing richer. In the pages that follow,
I've noted the sources that have been the most helpful to me in writing this book; due to space, the list must be regrettably partial. I've
included source information in English, though in some cases the
works were published in other languages, namely Ukrainian.

I relied on two works by Timothy Snyder, *The Reconstruction
of Nations: Poland, Ukraine, Lithuania, Belarus, 1569–1999* (Yale University Press, 2003) and *Bloodlands: Europe Between Hitler and Stalin*
(Basic Books, 2010), and Paul R. Magosci's *A History of Ukraine: The
Land and Its Peoples* (University of Toronto Press, 2010) to understand the general sweep of history in the region.

John-Paul Himka's *Galician Villagers and the Ukrainian National
Movement in the Nineteenth Century* (Macmillan, 1988) was an essential source in trying to bring to life the Galicia of the late nineteenth
and early twentieth centuries. Keely Stauter-Halsted's *The Nation in
the Village: The Genesis of Peasant National Identity in Austrian Poland,
1848–1914* (Cornell University Press, 2001) was also helpful. Samuel Koenig's ethnographic writings on Ukrainian Galicia, which
appeared in various sources in the 1930s and 1940s, chronicle the
culture's birth, marriage, child-rearing, and mortuary practices as
well as its beliefs about magic, the supernatural, the afterlife, and
the soul.

I sourced Austrian officials' colorful descriptions of Ukrainian
serfs from Franz A. J. Szabo's article "Austrian First Impressions of
Ethnic Relations in Galicia: The Case of Governor Anton von
Pergen," in *Polin: Studies in Polish Jewry* 12 (1999). Alison Fleig
Frank's *Oil Empire: Visions of Prosperity in Austrian Galicia* (Harvard
University Press, 2005) traces the brief but powerful role that the oil
industry played in Galicia. I relished the details of pre-WWII Gali-
cian life that were chronicled in two memoirs, Jan Slomka's *From
Serfdom to Self-Government: Memoirs of a Polish Village Mayor, 1842–
1927* (Minerva, 1941) and Michael Hrycyszyn's *God Save Me From*

My Friends and From My Enemies I'll Save Myself Alone: A Ukrainian Memoir (Vanguard, 2006).

Leonid Heretz's writings on Mshanets, Ukraine, particularly "The Formation of Modern National Identity and Interethnic Relations in the Galician Ukrainian Highlands: Some Findings from a Local/Oral History Project," in the *Journal of Ukrainian Studies* 33-4 (2008-2009), capture fine-grain details of rural western Ukrainian life. John-Paul Himka's article "Ukrainian-Jewish Antagonism in the Galician Countryside During the Late Nineteenth Century" in *Ukrainian-Jewish Relations in Historical Perspective*, edited by Peter J. Potichny and Howard Aster (Canadian Institute of Ukrainian Studies, 1988), provides an in-depth look at the complex relationship between Ukrainians and Jews in Galicia.

I am grateful to the trusting steward of Staryava's handwritten history, Y.I. Voyitiv's *The History of the Village of Staryava, Stariy Sambir Region, Lviv Oblast* (1989), who let me take it back to Truskavets for a few days circa 2014 and photocopy it so I could make use of its details. Other basic information on Staryava was drawn from the village's entry in the *History of the Cities and Villages of the Ukrainian SSR* (Ukrainian Soviet Encyclopedia of the Academy of Sciences of the USSR: 1968), the Polish Business Directories of the 1920s and 1930s, and the Polish censuses. I obtained the records from Staryava's branch of Prosvita as well as the village's cadastral maps from the Central State Historical Archives of Ukraine in Lviv. The Central Archives of Historical Records in Warsaw, Poland, holds the prewar registers of St. Paraskeva, my family's church in Staryava, from which I obtained crucial birth, death, and marriage information.

The two short biographies of Stefan Mazur came from Zenon Shandrovich's two-volume history on OUN-UPA in western Ukraine, *In Battle for the Freedom of Ukraine* (Leoprint, 2002). (I primarily accessed the book online at www.free-ukraine.com via a copy archived by the Wayback Machine in 2017.) The book also contains a memoir essay by Stepania Mazur (no relation, at least that I'm aware of), a contemporary of Stefan's who also belonged to Prosvita in Staryava and was recruited to OUN as a teenager.

I uncovered residence and employment documents from Stefan's time in Germany at the Arolsen Archives (formerly the International Tracing Service archive) at the U.S. Holocaust Memorial Museum. Ulrich Herbert's *Hitler's Foreign Workers: Enforced Foreign Labor Under the Third Reich* (Cambridge University Press, 1997), Karl Liedke's *Faces of Forced Labor: Poles in Braunschweig, 1939–1945* (Arbeitskreis Andere Geschichte, 1997), and Tetyana Lapan's article, "The Experience of Forced Laborers in Galician Ukraine," in *Hitler's Slaves: Life Stories of Forced Laborers in Nazi-Occupied Europe*, edited by Alexander von Plato, Almut Let, and Christoph Thonfeld (Berghahn Books, 2010), helped me imagine Stefan's time as a laborer in Germany.

Yosip Punko's transfer to Auschwitz and his subsequent incarceration and death at the Mauthausen concentration camp were illuminated by documents I found at the Arolsen Archives at the U.S. Holocaust Memorial Museum. Diemut Majer's *"Non-Germans" Under the Third Reich: The Nazi Judicial and Administrative System in Germany and Occupied Eastern Europe, with Special Regard to Occupied Poland, 1939–1945* (Johns Hopkins University Press, 2003) documents in extraordinary detail the oppressive, merciless atmosphere of German-occupied Poland. *Anatomy of the Auschwitz Death Camp* (Indiana University Press, 1998), edited by Yisrael Gutman and Michael Berenbaum; Danuta Czech's *Auschwitz Chronicle, 1939–1945* (Henry Holt, 1990); and Rudolf A. Haunschmied, Jan-Ruth Mills, and Siegi Witzany-Durda's *St. Georgen Gusen Mauthausen: Concentration Camp Mauthausen Reconsidered* (Gusen Memorial Committee, 2007) provide key details about the camps in which Punko was imprisoned.

Jan Tomasz Gross's *Revolution from Abroad: The Soviet Conquest of Poland's Western Ukraine and Western Belorussia* (Princeton University Press, 1988) provides a lively history of the Soviet occupations of western Ukraine. Alexander Statiev's *The Soviet Counterinsurgency in the Western Borderlands* (Cambridge University Press, 2010) was an essential source about the war, the Ukrainian auxiliary police, and OUN-UPA and its SB. Wartime memoirs I found helpful were Petro J. Potichnyj's *My Journey* (Litopys UPA, 2008), Stefan Petelycky's *In Auschwitz, for Ukraine* (Kashtan Press, 1999), and *The Diary of Samuel Golfard and the Holocaust in Galicia* by Wendy Lower (AltaMira Press, 2011).

Father Patrick Debois's *The Holocaust by Bullets: A Priest's Journey to Uncover the Truth Behind the Murder of 1.5 Million Jews* (St. Martin's Griffin, 2008), Yitzhak Arad's *The Holocaust in the Soviet Union* (University of Nebraska Press, 2009), and Karel C. Berkhoff's *Harvest of Despair: Life and Death in Ukraine Under Nazi Rule* (Belknap Press, 2004) provide quality overviews of the execution of the Holocaust in Ukraine. I accessed the Operational Situation Reports prepared by the Einsatzgruppen, the mobile Nazi killing squads, via http://www.holocaustresearchproject.org, for a grim, day-by-day window into the Holocaust in western Ukraine in 1941 and 1942. Interviews with Holocaust survivors held by the USC Shoah Foundation's visual history archive, particularly those with Herman Teicher and Ben Teicher, added a hyper-local perspective. Yad Vashem's Central Database of Shoah Victims' Names can be accessed online at yvng.yadvashem.org. Raisel Meltzak's testimony is online at the Voices of the Holocaust Project (https://voices.library.iit.edu/interview/meltzakR).

Martin Dean's *Collaboration in the Holocaust: Crimes of the Local Police in Belorussia and Ukraine, 1941–1944* (St. Martin's Press, 2000) details the functions — and complicity — of Ukrainian auxiliary police. Also helpful on this topic were Gabriel N. Finder and Alexander V. Prusin's "Collaboration in Eastern Galicia: The Ukrainian Police and the Holocaust," in *East European Jewish Affairs* 34, no. 2 (Winter 2004), Dieter Pohl's report for the Office of Special Investigations at the U.S. Department of Justice, *Ivan Kalymon, the Ukrainian Auxiliary Police and Nazi Anti-Jewish Policy in Lviv, 1941–1944* (2005), and David Rich's "Armed Ukrainians in Lviv: Ukrainian Militia, Ukrainian Police 1941 to 1942" in *Canadian-American Slavic Studies* 43, no. 3 (2014). I obtained Stefan Mazur's application to join the Ukrainian auxiliary police and the "Kolaborant" case file that detailed the allegations against him while serving in the police from the Rzeszow branch of Poland's Institute of National Memory.

Anne Applebaum's *Gulag: A History* (Doubleday, 2003), Lynne Viola's *The Unknown Gulag: The Lost World of Stalin's Special Settlements* (Oxford University Press, 2007), and Daniel Beer's *The*

House of the Dead: Siberian Exile Under the Tsars (Knopf, 2017) helped me understand the comparatively neglected special settlements within the history of Siberian exile. Oleksandr Pahirya's article, "Operation West in Western Ukraine in October 1947," published on Lviv's Territory of Terror Museum website, was one of the few comprehensive articles available on the event when I started researching it in the mid-2010s. I accessed several Soviet documents about the implementation of Operation West from the electronic archive of the Ukrainian Liberation Movement (http://arv.org.ua). The case files of the adult members of my family who were exiled — Rozalia Mazur, Anna Mazur Bandriwska, Ivan Mazur, and Andriy Bandriwsky — came from the Ministry of Internal Affairs in Lviv.

On the thorny topic of Ukrainian nationalism, Myroslav Shkandrij's *Ukrainian Nationalism: Politics, Ideology, and Literature, 1929–1956* (Yale University Press, 2015) was indispensable. Grzegorz Rossolinski-Liebe's *Stepan Bandera: The Life and Afterlife of a Ukrainian Nationalist: Fascism, Genocide, and Cult* (ibidem-Verlag, 2014) is an incisive study of the controversial OUN leader. Trevor Erlacher's *Ukrainian Nationalism in the Age of Extremes: An Intellectual Biography of Dmytro Dontsov* (Ukrainian Research Institute, 2021) helped me understand Ukrainian nationalism in relation to other nationalisms in Eastern Europe that developed around the same time. Serhiy Kudelia's paper at the 2011 Danyliw Research Seminar in Contemporary Ukrainian Studies, "The Impact of Collectivization on Insurgency Mobilization in Western Ukraine After World War II," chronicles how collectivization impacted UPA's operations after World War II formally ended.

The case files covering the wartime activities of Andriy Mazur and Stepan Mazur came from the Security Services Archives in Lviv, while the Ministry of Internal Affairs in Lviv holds Stefan Mazur's file that records his alleged activities as a member of OUN-UPA. Jeffrey Burds' scholarship, specifically "Gender and Policing in Soviet West Ukraine, 1944–1948," *Cahiers du Monde Russe*, 42/2-4 (2001) and "AGENTURA: Soviet Informants' Networks and the Ukrainian Underground in Galicia, 1944–1948," *East European*

Politics and Societies 11, no. 1 (Winter 1997) shed light on the day-to-day operations of OUN-UPA.

I relied on John-Paul Himka's groundbreaking *Ukrainian Nationalists and the Holocaust: OUN and UPA's Participation in the Destruction of the Ukrainian Jewry, 1941–1944* (ibidem Press, 2021) to understand the complex dynamics that led Ukrainians to participate in the Holocaust. Jared McBride's 2014 PhD dissertation, "'A Sea of Blood and Tears': Ethnic Diversity and Mass Violence in Nazi-Occupied Volhynia, Ukraine, 1941–1944," (University of California, Los Angeles), was also helpful in understanding these dynamics. Kai Struve's "The OUN(b), the Germans, and Anti-Jewish Violence in Eastern Galicia During Summer 1941," in the *Journal of Soviet and Post-Soviet Politics and Society*, no. 6 (Summer 2020) provides a clear-eyed accounting of the roles of various actors in the first violent summer of the Nazi occupation of western Ukraine.

Georgiy Kasianov's *Memory Crash: Politics of History in and Around Ukraine, 1980s–2010s* (Central European University Press, 2022) is a master work on Ukraine's complicated memory politics. I also benefitted from David R. Marples's *Heroes and Villains: Creating National History in Contemporary Ukraine* (Central European University Press, 1997). Per A. Rudling's article, "The OUN, the UPA, and the Holocaust: A Study in the Manufacturing of Historical Myths," in *The Carl Beck Papers in Russian and East European Studies*, no. 2107 (2011) looks at how OUN-UPA have been treated by recent Ukrainian governments. In 2022, the *Forward* updated its detailed list of monuments, streets, and plaques in Ukraine that honor individuals involved in OUN-UPA, the Ukrainian auxiliary police, and Ukrainian military units under the Nazis. It is available at https://forward.com/news/462916/nazi-collaborator-monuments-in-ukraine.

Ancestry.com gave me access to valuable data, including paperwork documenting Stepan, John, and Mike Mazur's journeys from Staryava to the United States, and the U.S. naturalization processes of John and Mike. The 1920, 1930, and 1940 U.S. censuses allowed me to track the Mazur household as it changed shape and moved around Cleveland. Ancestry also quickly served up documents that helped me get specific about birth, death, and marriage dates.

The websites of the Tremont History Project and Cleveland Historical and *Tremont: Cleveland, Ohio's Southside* by Paul Ziats (Merten Company, 1997) helped me paint a portrait of Cleveland's Southside neighborhood (now Tremont) during Mike's time there. Several documents I found at the Ukrainian Museum-Archives in Cleveland also helped with this task.

Finally, Rozalia Mazur's Alien File, held by U.S. Citizenship and Immigration Services, offered a surprisingly intimate window into my great-grandparents' thirty-two years of separation and Rozalia's one-way journey from Siberia to Cleveland.

UKRAINIAN VOICES

Collected by Andreas Umland

ibidem.eu